Live God LOUD

© Ron Luce

WORD PUBLISHING

NASHVILLE

A Thomas Nelson Company

D1115748

LIVE GOD LOUD

Published by Word Publishing, a unit of Thomas Nelson, Inc.,
P.O. Box 141000, Nashville, Tennessee 37214.

Published in association with the literary agency of
Alive Communications, Inc., 7680 Goddard Street, Suite 200,
Colorado Springs, Colorado 80920.

Copyright © 2000 by Ron Luce. All rights reserved.

No portion of this book may be reproduced, stored in a retrieval
system, or transmitted in any form or by any means—
electronic, mechanical, photocopy, recording, or any other—
except for brief quotations in printed reviews,
without the prior permission of the publisher.

Unless otherwise indicated, Scripture quotations used in this
book are from *The Holy Bible, New International Version.*
Copyright © 1973, 1978, 1984, International Bible Society.
Used by permission of Zondervan Bible Society.

Scripture quotations indicated NASB are from the *New American
Standard Bible* ®. Copyright the Lockman Foundation ©
1960, 1962, 1963, 1968, 1971, 1972, 1973, 1975, 1977.
Used by permission.

Scripture quotations indicated KJV are from the King James
Version of the Bible.

ISBN 0-8499-4281-0

Printed in the United States of America
00 01 02 03 04 05   PHX   9 8 7 6 5 4 3 2 1

Dedication

To my son *Cameron Townsend Luce.*
May my life demonstrate to you the teachings herein.

Live God LOUD

◎ Contents

v

‹ Contents ›

Acknowledgments

Thank you to *Greg Johnson* for all his hard work
making this book come together.
Also, thanks to *Brandi Arnold,*
Kristin Bown, Belinda Ball,
and *Stephanie Morrisett,*
who helped prepare the original manuscript.
Special thanks to *Juliana Diaz,*
who inspired the idea.

Live God
LOUD

Y ou know what loud is, right?

It's your stereo or headphones cranked to 10. It's your coach practically spitting in your face while making sure you hear the right instructions in the last few seconds of a game. It's your parents repeating a warning when they don't think you have your hearing aid turned up (or the TV is too loud). Whomever it comes from, *loud* means someone is trying to get your attention.

So what does it mean to "Live God Loud"?

Does it mean God's got ten BIG commandments He knows He's going to have to scream at you to get them through your thick head? Does it mean you have to live in total fear so as not to incur the anger of an invisible powerhouse who likes to squish little teenagers having fun? Or does it mean you must wear an obnoxious T-shirt to let the world know you're a religious fruitcake?

Nope. Nope. And nope.

It means you've taken the challenge to turn up the volume of a loving God in your life. That's what this book is going to help you accomplish. You might be someone who has been living God at 1 for a long time, barely above a whisper and certainly not loud enough to hear much of Him because of all the other voices screaming in your ear. If you're open to it, I'd like you to take the volume control of your choices and choose to turn God up. One . . . two . . . perhaps five notches. (Maybe ten!) How do you do that? The first thing you've got to do is realize that there IS a volume control for God in your life, and you CAN turn it up.

> ◄◄ *Many of your friends are not taking seriously the consequences of playing life at a 10 and God at a 1. They are fooling around with the things of the world that promise to overwhelm the still, small voice of God.*

You turn it up by turning the other voices—your other choices—down to a level that God says you can manage. And you turn it up by living God's Word a bit louder than you did yesterday.

Many of your friends are not taking seriously the consequences of playing life at a 10 and God at a 1. They are fooling around with the things of the world that promise to overwhelm the still, small voice of God. Even some of your Christian friends try to keep the volume of life just loud enough to fit in with the world, but not so loud that they can't fit in at church. And sadly, those volume choices do nothing but increase the noise of temptation that leads to a headache full of sin.

How about you? Have you made those same choices on the volume knob of God that you control?

Being a Christian means turning up the volume to God and letting Him begin to control the volume from the world that's constantly trying to crank a little louder. It's not superhuman effort God wants from you; it's better volume control choices. Of course God wouldn't say it exactly like this, but He's saying to you today, "Live Me loud and you can not even imagine the music you'll hear from heaven. Live Me loud and your life will play a melody that dozens, hundreds, perhaps thousands will be attracted to. Live Me loud and you won't ever have to regret the morning headaches of guilt and shame that are guaranteed if you're living the world loud. Live Me loud and we'll be the closest of friends in this life . . . and the next."

I've known hundreds of teens who want to live God loud only in times of crisis. They halfheartedly go to church and youth group but never take God seriously unless their backs are up against a wall. And I've known thousands of teens who truly want to live God loud but just don't know how to plug into His power and how to work the controls. They sometimes think living God loud means finding an emotional time at the altar during a retreat. During these mountaintop moments, the volume control to God is adjusted to 10 and the "feelings" are great. But feelings go away, and when they do, many teens go on an endless cycle of trying to get them back. It's an honest effort at living God loud, but most get tired of going back and forth trying to keep the volume at 10 through good feelings. I can't blame them. The Bible never says to live God loud with your feelings.

It is time to get honest about the issues that are causing teens like you to keep God at level 1. There is simply too much fun and fulfillment in living God loud. Again, that's what this book will help you do. You need real solutions for the real pressure and rough times you're facing. The answers to living God loud are found in the Word. The only way to turn up the volume on God is to turn up the volume on the Bible. This book may not be something to make you feel good about what you are doing, but it is a book that will show you how to turn down the volume in situations that cause Christian teens to fall on their faces. It is help for the specific issues that you are wrestling with.

You *do not* have to be the Christian teen who's constantly going back and forth in your walk with God. You can live God loud while you are young and never have to adjust that volume again. It is time to get plugged into the power from the Most High God and never let the world unplug it—ever!

As we draw closer to the end times, the complexity of the issues you face is increasing. Even if you've been in a church all of your life, God can relate to the problems you're facing on a daily basis. You no longer have to think, *If the Christian life is so great, then why can't I get it together? Why are so many things falling apart in my life? Where is God when all these things are happening to me?*

He's not in the woofer, tweeter, or bass; He's in the volume control. Is your hand poised to make some adjustments? Then let's go.

Section ONE

◎ *Becoming Spiritually Hungry*

Don't you get frustrated and annoyed when . . .

- ◎ you hear fingernails on a chalkboard
- ◎ you're behind an extra-slow driver on the freeway
- ◎ you're playing your best and the basketball referee is calling his worst
- ◎ someone takes the volume knob and makes it loud and quiet, loud and quiet, loud and quiet

Some things just get on your nerves. Does God get frustrated and annoyed when you take the volume control of your walk with Him and turn it up when camps and Sundays hit then turn it down nearly every other waking moment? Believe it or not, He doesn't. No, He's not too excited about these ups and downs, but He understands that when you're young, your daily walk with Him often resembles a roller coaster. Does He want you to stay that way, turning the volume up and down on a daily basis?

What do you think?

Wouldn't it be incredible to be living God *consistently loud* so . . .

- ◎ you wouldn't hit spiritual and emotional lows
- ◎ you wouldn't become indifferent toward God as you're living day by day

◎ you wouldn't be overcome by guilt because you "blew it again"

◎ people would see Christ through you without you telling them you're a Christian

You cannot be a "live God quiet" Christian and expect Him to bless your life. You have to blast through the tendency to take the "safe" route of living God at a 1 or the frustrating route of seeing God's volume in your life go from 1 to 7, from 2 to 8, from 3 to 9.

You might be young, but you are not too young to be serious in your pursuit of God. David, Josiah, Mark, and Timothy are all biblical examples of young people who were serious about God. You cannot go on praying a crisis prayer every time you get into trouble and hoping God will get you out of the mess. It would be far better to live God loud so you could hear His voice when He tells you how to avoid the messes in the first place.

This first section is written to help you keep the volume control at a higher level so you don't cave in to the emotional ups and downs—and the distractions—most Christian teens go through. The ultimate goal is to stay real with God. If you consistently apply these volume control techniques to your life, you will rarely live God at the lower numbers again.

◄◄ *You cannot be a "live God quiet" Christian and expect Him to bless your life. . . . You might be young, but you are not too young to be serious in your pursuit of God.*

Live God LOUD

Chapter 1 ◎ How Much of God Do You Want? Getting God's Full Meal Deal

Brad was on a constant search for something that would fill him up. He wanted more fun, so he hit every party he could on weekends. He wanted more adventure, so whenever he could ride a rapid or hunt with friends, he was gone. He wanted more thrills, and to him, thrills meant different combinations of alcohol and drugs. He wanted more happiness, so he went from girl to girl, thinking that finding the right one who could please him would bring him the answer. He had the world's volume at a constant 10, but he had no peace in his heart and no direction in his life. He'd occasionally go to a youth group or the local Campus Life, but the challenge to turn down the volume of doing things the world offered, things that couldn't last . . . well, to him, it didn't make sense. *Isn't life meant to be lived to the fullest?* he thought. *How can God make life exciting?*

We, as human beings, are hungry for something to fill the holes in our lives. We know that something around us needs to be lived loud and that it must be something that can be seen, touched, tasted . . . experienced!

What do you crave more than anything? What do you really want?

The Bible says in Matthew 5:6, "Blessed are those who hunger and thirst for righteousness, for they will be filled." This means you're blessed if you're hungry for God.

God makes it clear to us that we are all empty without His love and power inside. No matter how you look on the outside with the right clothes, the best physique, or the coolest car, if you aren't making the choices to live God loud, then your tank will always register empty.

Think about the last time you were hungry. I mean *really* hungry. All you could think about was food. Your mind created images of burgers, pasta, salad . . . Whatever makes you salivate, that's what you were thinking about.

A friend of mine took nine guys inner-tubing down a river in Oregon. For four hours they floated in wet suits while sitting in a tube going through cold, mountain-water rapids. They had left at 8:00 A.M., put in the river by 10:00, and for the next four hours floated twelve miles of gorgeous river. Inner tubes don't have convenient holders for coolers, so they had to forget about their stomachs.

As they waded out of the river, they were about as hungry as ten guys could be. But instead of hitting the first fast-food joint they could find on their way home, they decided to wait for the perfect restaurant: a buffet. The best buffet they knew about was ninety minutes away. Not a milepost marker went by that they didn't think about food. But they held out, and when they arrived at the restaurant, they were rewarded. Can you imagine

> ◄◄ *God makes it clear to us that we are all empty without His love and power inside. No matter how you look on the outside with the right clothes, the best physique, or the coolest car, if you aren't making the choices to live God loud, then your tank will always register empty.*

how much food ten guys can put away when they haven't eaten for seven or eight hours? You're right. The buffet didn't make a dime on those guys.

Jesus said we should be hungry for righteousness. This means we should be longing for every part of our life to be right in step with God. We should want God to smile on every part of what we do each new day. This includes our habits, attitudes, friends, free time, feelings, music, movies, school, family, and boyfriend or girlfriend.

Many young people who have been in church for a long time say, "I've been in church for years. I've prayed the prayer to receive Christ . . . Why am I not filled up?"

Jesus promised that you would be filled, not if you go to church, not if you go to youth group, not if you cry at the last night of camp every year, but only if you are *hungry* for Him and for righteousness.

Those ten guys who went down the river knew what hunger was. It was a craving.

To crave means to strongly want something that will satisfy a need. According to the dictionary, it's about "longing for and earnestly, intensely desiring to get a need fulfilled; an eagerness, an inclination, a passion." It is like you are so famished and thirsty that you devour greedily.

Are You Hungry?

Have you ever thought about what you crave the most? Our bodies tell us to crave things like what to eat and drink. Our friends tell us to crave things like what's cool to wear, drive, and listen to. Our inner passions tell us to crave what's pleasurable to the eyes and what feels good. The world tells us to crave fun and excitement, sports and competition, movies and video games, possessions and status.

What teenagers in America crave can be discerned from what they are putting into their minds and lives:

- ◎ The average teen by 12 to 17 years of age watches 23 hours of TV per week.[1]
- ◎ By the time teenagers finish high school, they will have spent 18,000 hours with the TV "curriculum" and only 12,000 hours on school curriculum.[2]
- ◎ By the time teenagers graduate, they will have listened to 10,500 hours of music;[3] seen 18,000 murders on TV;[4] seen an estimated 14,000 sexual references and innuendos per year on TV;[5] and viewed 100,000 beer commercials.[6]

These are just some of the things that are filling the minds and hearts of teens all over America and around the world. While the average teen may not see all of this as a lot of "junk food" for their head and heart, the perceptive teen—the one who desires to live God loud—will.

Though we all like an occasional burger, smothered pizza, or candy bar, the only thing that junk food gives us is the illusion of being full without the benefit of real nutrients. We feel full, but our body says we're still empty. Sure, we can live a long time on junk food—as many are doing—but we cannot *live well* with a constant diet of substances without nutrients.

The world offers so much junk food to you and me that it makes us forget to hunger for God. Our soul has the illusion of being filled, so we wind up thinking that we don't need the Bible. We become believers who say we love God, but we forget to hunger for more of Him! The result: We get so satisfied with mediocrity that we think we are doing pretty good as Christians. We forget to pursue our Savior passionately.

As Christians, if we live according to the diet the world wants us to have (the world's volume control) without a solid intake of great spiritual food, our relationship with God will at the very least be distracted, and at the most be destroyed.

Sarah is like a million other teen girls who go to youth group every week. She's watching all of the latest first-run movies, she's plugged into MTV, and she's reading *Teen People* and several other girls magazines. Once in a while, she'll tell me about one of the newest stars who has "thanked God" on some award show, or who "talked about heaven and angels on a talk show," or who "wore a cross in his latest music video." While her heart is looking for God in the world of celebrities, passing references to Him don't encourage her to live God loud. Instead, they simply help to justify her intake of "cool" stuff.

Has Sarah been brainwashed when she gets ideas on God and heaven from Hollywood and from popular music? Well . . . yes. But she doesn't even know it and wouldn't believe me if I told her. She has taken the "truth" from the world and, unfortunately, lives God and His Word at a volume of 1. It's unfortunate because volume 1 of God for her makes the Bible seem like a fairy tale while the world seems like reality. Even though her world consistently mocks God, she still doesn't have a clue that her brain is being programmed to keep the volume of God at the lowest levels possible.

I don't want to seem too hard on Sarah. She's a girl in process, not too much unlike you or someone you know. It's tough to live in the world without hearing—and to some degree believing—its noise. And learning discernment and making the choice to turn down the volume low enough to hear God happen at a different rate for each of us.

How long will it take you?

True, I don't know how perceptive you are, but my guess is you've seen firsthand how you or your friends have been on "world overload" and "God underload." Do you like the person you're becoming because of it? If not, it's time to . . .

Blow Some Chunks

If you have been eating all this junk, you need to throw up before your spiritual digestive system gets used to it.

You need to get it out of your life.

It's time to recognize the junk you feel full on, and start to make better food choices.

It's time to get rid of the garbage that has been filling your life and get hungry for God again.

How do you get the garbage out?

First, find a quiet place and try something unusual. Write down as many of the world's junk foods you can think of that you've been taking in. Anything that gives the feeling of satisfying a longing or need but isn't giving you nutrients needs to be identified. Not all are harmful, and I'm not asking you to become a nun or a monk. Just be real and honest by writing what you think *may* be blocking your ability to live God loud.

Second, ask God to help you pick which ones are doing you the most harm. If your list is long, you won't be able to get rid of everything, so don't think you can. But you can work on *one* thing, right? Sure you can.

Third, you've got to throw it up. You do that by asking God for forgiveness and repenting. *Repenting* means "turning around." True repentance means forsaking that sin that has been entangling you. If it's R-rated movies, quit going. If it's sensual music videos on MTV, quit watching. If it's pornography, guys, get rid of it today. If it's a few CDs in your collection that speak ill of God and promote a lifestyle that isn't right, get the hammer out. Girls, if it's one of the dozens of magazines that advertise "How to Get the Guy" on every issue, it's time to subscribe to *Brio*. There's only One Guy you should be pursuing to any great degree—Jesus Christ.

Fourth, find one friend who will help keep you headed in

the right direction. You can't try by yourself to get rid of things that are dulling your spiritual senses. Satan won't let you. The more you bend toward keeping things like this a secret, the less likely you'll succeed at even one commitment.

Are You Really Hungry?

Next, it's time to get hungry again for the things of God. Let me ask you some tough questions.

Have you ever been as hungry for God as David was? He wrote in Psalm 42:1, "As the deer pants for streams of water, so my soul pants for you, O God." Do you really long for God? It is time to take a drink of the right stuff. A full and quenching drink of the living God.

David wrote, "O God, you are my God, earnestly I seek you; my soul thirsts for you, my body longs for you, in a dry and weary land where there is no water" (Psalm 63:1). Do you earnestly want more of God in your life? A lot of people just go to church and then go home. They want to just barely make it to heaven. No wonder they are empty on the inside and seek to be filled by pursuing the things of the world. When was the last time you honestly sought God with all of your guts?

David wrote, "My soul yearns, even faints, for the courts of the LORD; my heart and my flesh cry out for the living God" (Psalm 84:2). He was passionately desiring to be as close as he possibly could to God. In your heart of hearts, do you want Him like that?

Psalm 34:8 says, "Taste and see that the LORD is good; blessed is the man who takes refuge in him." Are you satisfied with only a taste of God here and a taste there? Or do you know that there's a full meal deal that God is offering on a daily basis?

When I go to a restaurant, I usually order something different each time I'm there. I like variety. With food, of course, this is fine. With God, it's a recipe for failure and frustration.

Without realizing it, many Christians are "samplers." They "try" God at a camp, then they go back to their world and taste a little of everything else on the menu. They try a little alcohol, a few drugs, and moments of immorality. Unfortunately, they think they got all of God because they "tasted" what it was like *one time.* It may be time for you to *fill up* on Him. You see, if you just try a taste of God and the Christian life, you *won't* be fully satisfied and you *will* still be hungry for more. If you don't consistently go to His table to have more of Him, you will try to fill up on other things.

Things to Hunger For

Mark was raised in the church, said "the prayer" when he was five years old, and could read and memorize Scripture like no one else. But there was a *slight* problem. To him, Jesus was just a guy in white clothes and a beard. Things didn't get better through his grade-school years. He went to church to be with friends, but he left Jesus out of the picture entirely during his teen years. At fifteen, he knew *something* was missing. With hormones at full speed, he turned to girls. The void was filled . . . temporarily. He went to his first Acquire the Fire (ATF) conference at age seventeen. God got turned up to a 10, but only for a short period of time. Giving no attention to the Word, he went back to his old lifestyle of living the world loud.

Mark went to his second ATF when he was eighteen. By that time the emptiness and his sins were overwhelming him. In his own words, "I had become a hypocrite of the worst kind. The

---

◀◀ *Without realizing it, many Christians are "samplers." They "try" God at a camp, then they go back to their world and taste a little of everything else on the menu.*

music I filled my ears with spoke against my Creator. The movies I watched were filled with violence and nudity. I was so deep into it that I was able to block out God completely. I was so blind to my own sin that I could justify almost anything."

Through God's sovereignty, he hooked up with Teen Mania as a camp counselor. "During the training, I abstained from secular music and even fasted. God worked and worked in me. I learned to lean on God for everything. I was slowly being emptied so Christ could fill me." Today, God's voice rings loud and clear in Mark. "I long to read the Word of God and worship because it finally has meaning. Most of all, I long to pray because it isn't just a one-way communication. He is my reason for life because everything else is infinitely small compared to Him."

How's It Taste?

You won't hunger for something if it doesn't taste good. Consequently, God made sure that everything about following Him would taste awful, putrid, and be sure to gag you. *(Pause for effect.)*

Sometimes you've got to say it wrong to get it right.

Why would God say to hunger and thirst for Him and then make it taste bad? The answer? He wouldn't. Then why do so many teens think that if you're seeking after God it's the social kiss of death, the end of fun as you know it, and the beginning of a destined life as a sign-carrying religious nut?

Bad information.

A poor example.

One "negative" experience.

Or, like Mark, more of a desire to live the world loud and keep God's volume at a low level.

Whatever happens, the word gets around. The result is that not many truly hunger and thirst for God.

I believe that it's simply an information gap. People haven't been told all of the truth about the truth, so they naturally are afraid of it. What is the truth?

To hunger for God is to feel a little empty when the Word of God—God's truth in the Bible—isn't ingested on a regular basis.

To hunger for God is to want nothing but God's best in life and therefore want His guidance day by day.

To hunger for God is to admit that you can't love people on your own power, so you need to have the love of God burning in your heart.

To hunger for God is to have a consistent and powerful urge to understand more of His character so you can know and love Him more.

To hunger for God is to have the desire to want to be used by Him, somehow knowing that being involved in the things that God cares about—people—will bring more fulfillment than any other job ever could.

To hunger for God is not to understand all of the mysteries of prayer, but to want to know how to commune with Him day by day, hour by hour, minute by minute.

To hunger for God is to be sensitive to sin and to hate it in our own life.

To hunger for God is to have an intense desire to see miracles every day. God is still in the business of miracles, so we should always be ready to watch Him in action.

As you can clearly see, hungering for God is a journey, not something you can acquire next week just because you want to. Deep hunger pangs don't happen all at once; they come upon you slowly. And when we hunger for God, what does Jesus say will happen? "We *will* be satisfied" (see Matthew 5:6).

When I was a teen, *I was hungry!* I went so crazy about seeking Him that I read the entire Bible in six weeks. Some of you reading these pages can take the same challenge and do it too!

Others recognize your hunger but don't think you're starving yet, so you want to take it slower. While this way will eventually get you to your destination, it will take a lot of precious time. So don't delay.

Are You Desperate?

If you've ever sat through your "parents' hour" of watching the tube (the news), you've probably viewed pictures of famine that has broken out in countries around the world. I saw one feature that centered on fathers who wanted to work to get food for their wives and children, but no jobs were available. Finally the men began to rob and steal from others. They were not common criminals; they were just hungry. I even heard about a gang of men who stole powdered milk from an orphanage to get food for their own children. These men were desperate!

Are you desperate for God like that?

Are you willing to do whatever it takes to find Him? I've seen hundreds of starving children in India. Many of them beg in the streets all day long just trying to get food to live. However, in the same country, there are those who will take a whole platter of nicely diced vegetables and offer them to an idol. They will place the vegetables before the idol and let them lie there and rot as a sacrifice to a "god" who doesn't exist. They could eat the food and be healthy themselves or feed it to their own starving children, but instead they just let it rot.

It seems like a lot of starving Christians do the same thing. They have plenty of opportunities to eat the Word of God. The pastor or youth leader is preaching with all his heart. What's going on in the crowd? Teens tune out or sit there and write notes to their friends. God longs to feed them, but they refuse to eat. Any one of them could read the Bible, listen to tapes, and ask their leaders questions if they really wanted to learn more.

Instead, some choose to starve to death spiritually. Though they want the appearance of spirituality by doing occasional good things or going to Christian events, they forget to hunger for God. They want God's blessing, but do they want *Him*?

It's Time for a Feast

The Bible says, "Man does not live on bread alone but on every word that comes from the mouth of the LORD" (Deuteronomy 8:3). You cannot really be alive until you get God's Word in you. Physical bread cannot satisfy a hungry heart. Jesus said, "I am the bread of life. He who comes to me will never go hungry, and he who believes in me will never be thirsty" (John 6:35).

If you want real life, you have to have real bread.

God promises to fill you if you will just hunger for righteousness. If you are tired of feeling like an empty person or an empty Christian, get hungry for Him. He will fill you with Himself, and you can take that to the bank!

> ◄◄ *God promises to fill you if you will just hunger for righteousness.*

Live Loud
ACTION

Pray a prayer of repentance to get all the garbage out of your life that has been filling your mind and your heart. Next, do something to begin to fill yourself with God and His Word. Make a commitment to turn up the volume of God's Word in your life by reading one, two, or more chapters a day for thirty days. See if God doesn't meet you there and show you what living Him loud really means.

Live Loud
THOUGHT

"Seek first his kingdom and his righteousness, and all these things will be given to you as well" (Matthew 6:33).

Live God LOUD

Chapter 2 ◎ Are You Alive?
Taking Your Spiritual Pulse

Sixteen-year-old Kathy lived for camps and retreats. Though she appeared to be a strong Christian girl with good morals, she was a "mountaintop Christian." When she got away from her home and the crowd, she had the boldness of the apostle Paul and the heart of Mother Teresa. In her free time she could always be seen reading the Bible or some other Christian book. And whenever an invitation to make any type of stronger spiritual commitment was given, she was the first to stand or kneel or come forward.

Back in the real world, the Christian life was a struggle. Her home life wasn't too stable because her dad lived in another state and her mom wasn't a believer. And she had this one girlfriend who was in the more popular crowd. Invitations to parties and introductions to non-Christian guys constantly kept Kathy on the razor's edge of temptation.

There is no doubt Kathy genuinely met God at the mountaintop, but most mature Christians know that grass doesn't grow at the mountaintop; it grows in the valley. Peak experiences are needed to give us full-blown glimpses of God, but a "living God loud" faith is nourished in our *daily* volume control choices.

If you've been around the church for any length of time, you know what it means to be hyped-up for God. Camps and retreats are wonderful. But don't use them to get your emotions all stirred up; use them as marking a moment in time when God can touch your heart.

To be honest, peak experiences with God are good. Everyone needs them. We should all be more passionate about our faith. And the truth is, not many leave a retreat hoping to crash and burn when they get home. The problem comes when they discover that the feelings have diminished. The really immature Christians think God has left them, while others tend to go on the search for the next chance to get a few "spiritual goose bumps." When this happens too many times, the goose bumps—not the Savior—become the focus of their spiritual life.

Living God loud, then soft, loud, then soft is not what a normal Christian life is supposed to be about. It is not about whether you are stirred up or bored to tears. The Bible says that Jesus came that we "may have life, and have it to the full" (John 10:10b). He did not come to stir us up emotionally, but to give us life.

How can you tell if you have that real life inside you? Second Corinthians 13:5 says, "Examine yourselves to see whether you are in the faith; test yourselves." I talk with thousands of teenagers every week, and this is a truth: There are a lot of people who are walking around with living bodies on the outside but who are dead on the inside. More accurately, they are dry on the inside—lonely, empty, weary, and spiritually exhausted. Of course, all of us know people who have never given their life to the Lord who are just like this. They act like they are living— they're doing their best—but on the inside they're dying. The only way their hearts will "come alive" is if they give them to Jesus. The problem is that a lot of Christian teens who *have* given their lives to the Savior still seem dry and dead. That is why they keep trying to get an emotional high at events—intentionally and sometimes unintentionally. But an emotional high is an incomplete substitute for the real life God wants to fill us with.

Ed became a Christian in his sophomore year of high school. Though he was already a top athlete, you could see his stature change as he grew in his faith. He turned from a shy kid to someone who had confidence. He didn't have to compete with everyone to be the best because he had discovered who he was in Christ. As his insecurities faded, his boldness grew. Not in an obnoxious way, but in a natural, easygoing style. He intentionally went outside of his jock clique to make friends with everyone. Ed soon saw dozens of friends come to faith in Christ because like Jesus he "grew in wisdom and stature, and in favor with God and men" (Luke 2:52).

As Christians, we ought to be the most alive people our friends will ever meet. When our spiritual maturity grows and our confidence in who God made us to be takes root, how we carry ourselves—and even the look in our eyes—ought to reflect something supernaturally real inside of us. Why should this be the norm?

First, God has forgiven us. Not just in this life, but for eternity! Because of what Jesus did on the cross, our hearts are clean. Because of what the Spirit can do on a daily basis, our hearts can *stay* clean.

Second, God has given us a future. Our past is forgotten. We are sons and daughters of the God who created the universe, our world, and the flesh-and-blood bodies we look at every day in the mirror! If God is going to go to the trouble of making us, He's not going to leave us without a future or a hope.

Third, we can hear God's voice! We are not like dead people who have no sensitivity to the world. And we're not like those who reject Jesus and God's direction for their lives. We have a Father who loves to speak if we will only listen. When our thoughts become His thoughts, God speaks. When we give attention to His Word, He speaks. When we seek the advice of godly Christian leaders, He speaks.

Fourth, though temptation is all around—and sin *seems* fun for a season—the Holy Spirit has put within us a deep-down desire to live a pure and holy life. Though our flesh still wages a war with our renewed and regenerated spirit, God says "we are more than conquerors through him who loved us" (Romans 8:37). Galatians 2:20 says, "I have been crucified with Christ and I no longer live, but Christ lives in me. The life I live in the body, I live by faith in the Son of God, who loved me and gave himself for me." And Jesus promises, "My grace is sufficient for you, for my power is made perfect in weakness" (2 Corinthians 12:9).

We can live this life because His power lives inside us!

The Question of the Moment

Do you have this kind of life inside you? And if the seed is there, is it growing? Here are a few ways to check your spiritual barometer to see if you are moving in the right direction:

Are your roots deep? We know from the parable of the sower (see Matthew 13) that our roots must be deep if we want to stay alive. If you want your tree to grow (your spiritual tree), you have to have deep roots in the Lord.

A tree must have at least one deep taproot to keep the water coming to the rest of its branches. If it does not, during times of drought, the tree will die. The same is true for you. Your roots must be deep in God's Word so that when you don't have those "hype times," you still have life in you.

Having deep roots in God's Word doesn't mean you own four Bibles and your parents have twelve. It doesn't mean you can name fifty-six out of the sixty-six books of the Bible. And it doesn't mean you made it to your small-group Bible study seventeen weeks in a row. Growing deep roots happens when you put the Word of God in your heart and mind. "Blessed is the man who does not walk in the counsel of the wicked or stand in the way of sinners or sit in the seat of mockers. But his delight is in the law of the LORD, and on his law he meditates day and night. He is like a tree planted by streams of water, which yields its fruit in season and whose leaf does not wither. Whatever he does prospers" (Psalm 1:1–3).

If you meditate on God's Word . . .

TIME-OUT!

Quick definition of *meditate*: To me, it is when I turn my mind (sometimes forcing it) to think God's thoughts. I change the way I think to the way God thinks. To do that, I must know how God would think, so I'm constantly reading His Word to find out.

TIME IN.

. . . He will give you real life in your heart. You can't completely understand it with your mind. But the truth is, when you get His Word in your mind, and you meditate on it like a cow chews his cud, He gives you an unending burst of LIFE!

It is time to get serious about reading the Bible. Every single day, don't just read a few verses; memorize at least one passage of what you read. Take a passage and chew on it all day long, every single day.

What about reading through the whole Bible? Though the Bible can look intimidating, it's actually fascinating. There's adventure, history, songs, and best of all, the full counsel of God. Any question that relates to His character, His plan, or His blueprint for living an abundant life can be answered between

> ◄◄ Some Christians try to make you feel obligated to share the gospel with other people. But the fact is that if you really have that life burning inside you, you will not be able to keep it to yourself.

those covers. If you get serious about growing your roots deep in the Word, you will *constantly* have real life.

Are you nourished? Some people eat all the time but are not healthy. They eat, but because they eat junk food, they are weak and sickly.

Many Christians are like this. They go to church and even read their Bibles. But because they do not take seriously what they read, or what they hear, they are malnourished. They think that because they do the activity, they will be healthy. They wonder why they keep falling so easily into sin and bad habits. They go through the spiritual activities, but they don't have any spiritual LIFE bursting in their heart.

Believe it or not, one great way to get this spiritual nutrition is to fast. The idea is that you do not eat physically, but you do eat spiritually. In fact, you pig out on God! A fast is really a feast! Jesus said in Matthew 6:16, "When you fast . . ." not *if* you fast. In other words, He expects us to fast. It is a time of getting away from everything and everyone to get tight with God and let Him give you nutrients to live on.

Are you reproducing? You don't have to force, trick, or beg an apple tree to produce apples. It just does because it is a living apple tree. Because it's alive, it does it naturally. Your biology teacher would agree: Anything alive reproduces itself.

Have you reproduced the life of God inside you and given it to someone else? Are you bearing good fruit?

Some Christians try to make you feel obligated to share the gospel with other people. But the fact is that if you really have that life burning inside you, you will not be able to keep it to yourself.

Nobody should have to beg you or make you feel guilty before you tell others about Jesus Christ. In fact, if you have this burning life, it will naturally come out, just as an apple tree naturally gives apples. People should be asking you to shut up because you are talking about Him so much! Jesus said, "I am the vine; you are the branches. If a man remains in me and I in him, he will bear much fruit; apart from me you can do nothing" (John 15:5). If you are really alive, you will be bearing fruit and reaching others for Jesus.

Are your branches dead? The final thing that you can do to check your spiritual pulse is simply to check your branches. Look at your life and ask yourself, "Do I have any dead stuff on me?" The Bible says, "For the wages of sin is death" (Romans 6:23). That means that if there is any dead stuff in your life, you must have let sin in there.

Jesus said, "My Father . . . cuts off every branch in me that bears no fruit, while every branch that does bear fruit he prunes so that it will be even more fruitful" (John 15:1b–2).

The way a farmer gets rid of dead branches on his vines is to cut them off. That is exactly how we get rid of sin in our lives. We must cut it off. Sin kills you! It snuffs the vitality right out of your Christian life. Some Christians wonder why it is so hard to really hear from God. When we let sin in, we let death in. We can go to church every week and read our Bibles all the time, but if we let sin take root instead of the Lord, we let death in. That's why it's easy to go to church but still not feel alive on the inside. Once you cut the dead branches off, however, you will feel the freedom of real forgiveness and real LIFE!

Live Loud
ACTION

How do you cut off the dead branches of sin? Repent and ask forgiveness. Do not ever do it again. Think of every dead branch in your life right now. Take some time to ask God to forgive you. Ask God to pour the LIFE of His forgiveness into you this very moment.

Live Loud
THOUGHT

Let us "go, and sin no more," just like Jesus told the woman caught in her sin (John 8:1–11 KJV). Let us be the ones who show this world what real LIFE is all about. You should be the most ALIVE person anyone has ever met. Begin TODAY!

Live God LOUD

Chapter 3 ◎ Who's in Charge?
The Lordship of Jesus Christ

As a wild-living sixteen-year-old, I stumbled into church one day and it suddenly hit me: *God WAS real!* And if He was really alive, then He must have some sort of character . . . and probably some sort of plan for my life. I gave up my old life, old friends, and old way of thinking and gave myself completely to God. It didn't take long for me to see that God loved me, was thrilled I was one of His kids, and wanted to live His life through me. That's when I got fired up about living for God. I decided that the only fun and serious way to live the Christian life was to seek Him, submit to Him and His Word . . . and make Him Boss (Lord) of all of my actions.

Many young Christians find it easy to say they want to live for Jesus. They like the idea of heaven and spiritual gifts, and they love to scream His name loudly at youth conferences. The problem is: What happens when no one is around to see your excitement but the Lord? God knows it's great to be excited about Him in a group of other like-minded believers, but He wants to know if you're going to be serious about Him the rest of the week. Notice I said *serious,* not *excited.*

Did you know that the Bible never says you're to be excited about Jesus?

It says to take up your cross and follow. It says that following Him will mean going against the crowd. It says that if you want to be great, you've got to be willing to be a servant. But it never says "get pumped for God." Chasing after excitement is like chasing after the wind. You can never hold on to it long enough for it to do you any good. While you cannot keep your excitement forever, you can keep your commitment forever.

Commitment means understanding Who's in charge. If you want to stay in charge, fine. But realize that is not what God says is best for you. When He comes into your heart, He doesn't just want a small corner of it. He wants it ALL. You can't "sorta" jump out of an airplane. You can't "sorta" be a champion race-car driver. You can't "sorta" be serious about your high-school studies if you want to get into Harvard. You can't "sorta" be serious about being a Division I basketball player.

And you can't "sorta" let Jesus Christ be Lord.

What does it mean to allow Jesus to be your Lord? We may hear thousands yell, "Jesus is Lord" at a rally, but the voices who scream it are not always the lives who are living it. It is time for us to stop making a lot of noise about it and just do it: Submit to the lordship of Jesus Christ.

Why, you ask? Good question.

Because of Our Love for God

Matthew 22:37 says that you should "love the Lord your God with all your heart and with all your soul and with all your mind." I'm talking about loving God with all that you are, with everything you have inside of you. This is serious Christianity.

To love Him is to love His ways (how He does things), even when you do not understand everything about every situation. It's believing in your heart, "God, I know Your Word is true. Even though I don't understand why, I'm going to do it anyway because I love You and trust You."

Jesus said, "If you love me, you will obey what I command" (John 14:15). I believe this passage is true not only as it relates to our morals but also as it relates to the plans God has for us.

Colleen knew in her heart that God wanted her to go to Russia for a summer mission trip. The problem: finances. Not only didn't she have money for the trip, but her daily living account was low as well. That was unexpected, and it really shook her up. She had no clue where the money was going to come from. That night, she went on a run with another intern who was two months behind in her account but was standing in faith for that and for her total trip cost for Hong Kong.

"I was amazed at her faith," Colleen said. "God used that encounter to break me. I got serious about my desire to obey Him and told God how much I wanted to follow Him to Russia. A peace came over me and I just knew I was going. I even started telling people I was going, though I had no plane ticket and no money. I called my church and sent out a mass e-mail to everyone I knew. I began planning for my trip even though I still needed about $4,600.

"Over the next two weeks I fought so hard against Satan. He threw every doubt and fear at me. I continued to cry out to God and stand in faith. One week before my trip was to begin, I was

◄◄ *Moving out on faith—even when it's difficult—is our opportunity to demonstrate our love for God. We cannot simply do lip service and tell Him we love Him. We have to be ready.*

reading 1 John 5 where it talks about whatever we ask, according to God's will, we will receive. I stood on that. I told God that I knew it was His will that I go on this trip and that my finances would come in. The next day I received an e-mail from some friends who said they felt God put it on their heart to pay for my entire trip cost. My church agreed to pay up my daily living account. After that, more money just came pouring in. I was blessed beyond measure. And because of how greatly He blessed me, I was able to bless others."

Moving out on faith—even when it's difficult—is our opportunity to demonstrate our love for God. We cannot simply do lip service and tell Him we love Him. We have to be ready. When God's timing puts a situation in our midst—like Colleen talked about—we have to be ready to show Him we love Him.

Matthew 22:37 isn't about doing good works to get God to love us. He already loves us. But we obey Him as an outgrowth of our love for Him and for all He's done. Not out of compulsion, but from a heart that desires to return a small portion of the matchless love He's already given us.

What Does Loving God Look Like?

Our culture throws the word *love* around so much that it's hard to know what it means. For example, when we are into our first few bites of our favorite pizza, it would be normal to say to anyone listening, "I love pizza." We have strong feelings of attraction to someone of the opposite sex, so we assume it must be love. We practice our favorite sport four to six hours a day, so we show by our actions—and probably our words—that we love the sport. By the time we get around to saying (or thinking) that we love God, we have such an incomplete definition of love that we think it's the same thing.

Make no mistake: According to Jesus, loving God means

obeying His commandments and faithfully submitting to His lordship.

I know what you might be thinking at this point: *Why would I want to give all of my life to Someone I won't be able to see in this lifetime? What if it's not true? Won't I miss out on a lot of fun?* Fair questions. But there are huge advantages to being out of control and allowing God to be in control:

Spiritual LIFE. Romans 6:23 says, "For the wages of sin is death, but the gift of God is eternal life in Christ Jesus our Lord." Did you know that when you sin—if it remains unconfessed—you're earning wages? You are, and it's not minimum wage, it's maximum: spiritual death. That's not only a bad day's wage, it's most definitely a bad wage for eternity. And in case you're wondering, it's not physical death this passage is talking about; it's separation from God forever. And if your sin hasn't been paid for by Jesus (something that happens when you trust Christ to forgive your sins), death is the result.

If you're a Christian while you are allowing sin to take root in your life, your heart starts to get cold. Loneliness, confusion, lack of direction, even depression are a few of the consequences. You dry up on the inside. If you live in sin, your life and spirit can shrivel up to nothing. However, if you live a godly life, you will have real life on the inside! Jesus came to give us life, but we will not have it if we play games in our walk with Him.

Romans 6:16 says, "Don't you know that when you offer yourselves to someone to obey him as slaves, you are slaves to the one whom you obey—whether you are slaves to sin, which leads to death, or to obedience, which leads to righteousness?" That means that if you obey—and follow—sinful desires, you become a slave to those desires. Many Christians are in partial slavery. They say they love God, but they keep on obeying sinful desires. They wonder why it is so hard to enjoy God and to hear from Him, yet they refuse to get all of their life in submission to Him.

The word *Lord* means: boss, chief, the guy you report to, the dude in charge of your life. Got the idea? Saying we are committed to the Lord but doing our own thing is a joke we are playing only on ourselves. If you know you're having troubles keeping a consistent walk with Christ, then you probably need look no further than examining who's got control of the volume knob on making the world loud or living God loud.

Look at it this way: If you take drugs, then you are submitting control of your life to them. If you drink alcohol, then you are a slave to a liquid that influences how you think. If you follow your hormones and get into immorality, you are a slave to those hormones.

Freedom. Jesus promised to set us free from this slavery to sin. John 8:36 says, "So if the Son sets you free, you will be free indeed." Satan cannot boss you around anymore!

When you really submit to Him, He starts making everything work together for your good (see Romans 8:28). Life starts making sense again.

Shawn grew up with a mom who believed in "free love." A parade of men became his temporary "dads." With no role model and little adult stability, he did what he saw. In high school, he used one girl after another. Outgoing and good-looking, he always had friends to see, parties to go to, and another high to experience. He was invited to an evening Campus Life meeting where a speaker talked about sex. The message cut him right to the heart. He suddenly realized he had been abusing God's gift. Though he didn't even know God, he instinctively knew that what he had seen—and what he was doing—was wrong.

Shawn kept coming and soon turned his life over to Jesus Christ. Slowly and sometimes painfully, he threw off the old lifestyle to embrace the Savior. Thought changes led to behavior changes . . . which led to his friends asking a lot of questions (and many becoming Christians). The rest of the story is a testimony to God's goodness. Shawn went to Bible college, entered the ministry, and is now the pastor of a church of six hundred. A life that could have wound up going in the exact opposite direction was miraculously changed because the Son set Shawn free as he chose to allow Christ to determine the course of his life.

Do you see how the pain and sting of sin in our lives can be taken away as we bring every area of our life to Him?

He Demands That We Submit to His Lordship

Jesus said, "Not everyone who says to me, 'Lord, Lord,' will enter the kingdom of heaven, but only he who does the will of my Father who is in heaven" (Matthew 7:21). If Jesus really is our boss, why don't we obey Him? It would be like having a job at McDonald's and going to Burger King and saying, "Hi, boss, how are you doing?" He would say, "You don't even work here, so why are you calling me boss?" You can say "boss" all you want, but if you don't work there, he is not your boss. You can call Jesus your Lord all day long, but if you don't submit to Him, He is not your Lord.

In fact, you do not have the right to call Him your Lord unless you have submitted everything to Him. Paul said it this way: "You are not your own; you were bought at a price" (1 Corinthians 6:19b–20a). He figured that Jesus had bought him, so He owned him. That is what happens when we give our lives to Jesus—He takes full ownership. We no longer have the right to say what we are going to do or where we are going to go.

> ◄◄ *You can call Jesus your Lord all day long, but if you don't submit to Him, He is not your Lord.*

You may not like to think of it this way, but being connected to God is like joining the army. As long as you are enlisted, your leaders have the right to give out the orders. The reason they want strict obedience is they're preparing you for war, and at critical times in battle anything less than your willingness to obey your leaders could cost the life of a fellow soldier—or you. God's army is more intense because the stakes are higher and the foe is so strong that even Jesus called him "the ruler of this world" (John 12:31 NASB).

Jesus is not a drill sergeant who tries to get you to obey by intimidating you or screaming in your face. He cares about what you do and who you are. He knows that your actions will sometimes betray which army you're in, but if He has your heart he knows you will want to live God loud on a continual basis. Where your heart is, your actions will usually follow.

Making Christ the true Lord of your life means that you desire submission to what He wants in every part of your life. Jesus showed us a great example of how to live a submitted life. The Bible says, "Although he was a son, he learned obedience from what he suffered" (Hebrews 5:8). It also says, "He himself suffered when he was tempted" (Hebrews 2:18). Jesus knew what it was like to be tempted, to want to do something sinful. But because He was living His Father loud, He always said, "No way! I can't do that; I'm the Son of God!"

Jesus suffered when He was tempted the same way you and I suffer. Our battle is with sin that wages war inside of us. It's a struggle in our will to say no, and this is where we suffer. The Bible says Jesus learned obedience because EVERY TIME He suffered from that battle in the mind, He said NO! He learned obedience because EVERY TIME He got a chance, He turned it down and He obeyed His Father. Paul describes how Jesus even became obedient to death (see Philippians 2:8).

The great thing is that God gives us the same power today!

The Bible says in Titus 2:11–12, "For the grace of God that brings salvation has appeared to all men. It teaches us to say 'No' to ungodliness and worldly passions, and to live self-controlled, upright and godly lives in this present age." Every time you get tempted, you need to remember that God has given you the power to say NO! NO! NO! You are not a slave to sin any longer! He has set you free!

How to Get Out of Slavery

There are two steps to getting out of slavery to sin. And, remember, a *little* slavery is still bondage. You don't have to be a drug addict to be enslaved to sin.

The first step is something I've covered already but that needs repeating: to humbly ask God's forgiveness. First John 1:9 says, "If we confess our sins, he is faithful and just and will forgive us our sins and purify us from all unrighteousness." All of us know how good it feels to be forgiven, so asking usually isn't a real problem. It's the next step that is more challenging.

The second step is to repent. This is not the same as asking for someone's forgiveness. And it doesn't mean that you go and cry at the altar for an hour or two. Like I said earlier, to repent means to change your mind about something. To slam on the brakes and turn around. It means that you put your foot down and decide that you will no longer do the same things you have been doing. That you're sick of the choices you've been making and truly want to get away from circumstances that cause you to keep falling into the same rut.

Andrew was a Christian senior in high school who knew that drinking was wrong, but he'd go to parties with his friends to be the "designated driver." Good and noble. But within a month he was pulled into trying just one glass of beer . . . then another, then another. His testimony for the Lord and all of his good intentions were shot. He wanted to get out of his rut, but he realized that would mean he'd have to quit going to parties, something that would likely cost him his friends. After nearly getting into a car accident, he finally came to his senses. First he asked God for forgiveness, then he informed his buddies he was going to quit partying and start going to his youth group's Friday bashes after football games. Andrew turned around. He was committed to changing, and it cost him all but one of his friends. One saw the stand Andrew took and asked if he could come along to his youth group. A month later, Andrew's friend became a Christian.

True repentance doesn't always have this type of happy ending. Sometimes no one follows. But doing the right thing is its own reward. The devil has no right to tell you what to do. God has given you the power to say no, and that is exactly what you do when you repent. Believe it or not, repenting is a time to rejoice because you realize that you are no longer a slave! You are free, and you exercise your freedom by walking away from sin.

Live Loud Action

You have the volume knob of freedom right at your fingertips. It is time to turn up that volume by asking forgiveness, then turn it up a little louder by repenting. Find a scratch piece of paper and a pencil and make a list right now of the things in your life that you need to get rid of, the things of which you need to repent. Make the list, repeat it back to God out loud, then tear up the paper. Psalm 103:10–12 says, "He does not treat us as our sins deserve or repay us according to our iniquities. For as high as the heavens are above the earth, so great is his love for those who fear him; as far as the east is from the west, so far has he removed our transgressions from us." From this moment forward, you are FREE!

Live Loud THOUGHT

"Repent, then, and turn to God, so that your sins may be wiped out, that times of refreshing may come from the Lord, and that he may send the Christ, who has been appointed for you—even Jesus" (Acts 3:19–20).

Live God
LOUD

Chapter 4 ◉ Is It a Book . . . or Is It Jesus? Developing Consistent Quiet Times

To live God loud, to keep the volume of His voice at a 10, there is no mistaking one fact: You have to get quiet with Him on a daily basis and let His Word speak to you. In a 24/7 volume 10 world, you need to consistently hear God speak, and His voice is heard loudest in quiet.

Unfortunately, for many teens (and adults!), getting quiet means a one-way ticket to dreamland. And it's not too hard to understand why. Between TV, Walkmans, radios, phones, video games, and computers wired into the Internet with chat rooms and instant messages . . . life's volume is always hovering between 9 and 10, except when it's time for sleep city. I know a lot of kids who don't even turn the world down when homework stares them in the face—and they seem to do just fine! Being raised on the latest technology has made it difficult to see the value in getting quiet and listening to the Father. Most would say it's important . . . but almost impossible to do.

If you've been around the church for any length of time, you've heard it preached a zillion times that quiet time with God is one of the best ways to nourish your relationship with Him. I'd agree. It's essential for a growing Christian no matter what century or decade God has put you in. I've known thousands of Christian teens who have made genuine commitments to spend more time reading God's Word and less time on the constant buzz of electronic technology. Their commitment seemed so real at the altar. There they were, crying their eyes out to God, making promises they knew they would keep. If that moment could only last forever . . .

But one thing happens every day that is just too tough to ignore: 6:00 A.M.!

You have your Bible open and, well, it's odd. You don't feel God's presence at all, but at the same time there is a special feeling of holiness and majestic wonder that you're actually up early trying to connect with the invisible God. Most every other person you know is still sawing logs, but you're up early to capture the joy of reading that Book. That Book that was written two and three thousand years ago. After a couple of minutes, out of the corner of your eye, you spot your pillow. It's calling your name. At first you ignore it and redirect your eyes to that ancient Book that doesn't come close to resembling the MTV Web site. The voice of slumber grows louder, and your eyelids grow heavier. Soon you're convinced it's more holy to pray than to read. "And I'll just get comfortable with my head on that pillow over there, so I can rest in the Lord."

Zonk! You're out like a light, and you won't be disturbed until you hear your mom's voice—the same voice you're certain she bought at Kmart—telling you you're late for school. Suddenly, all of your commitments and good intentions are washed away for

⏮ *The problem with making quiet time a priority isn't a shortage of good intentions or commitments made. It's our attitude about what we're doing. Are we spending time with a BOOK, or are we spending time with JESUS?*

another day. You feel like a holy failure, but you keep trying. Eventually, however, you conclude that quiet times are a myth unless you were born in the '50s, and you've suddenly gone days and weeks without ever cracking the Book or bothering to pray.

That's when it's easy to think God has left you. That's when you find yourself wondering if you're still a Christian. And that's when you take the easy route and continue living the world at a 10 and God at a 1, falling into temptation and doing things that don't honor God.

Grab a New Attitude

The problem with making quiet time with God a priority isn't a shortage of good intentions or commitments made. It's our attitude about what we're doing. Are we spending time with a *book,* or are we spending time with *Jesus?*

Even if we are convinced we're taking the time for the *holy-awesome-most-important-book-in-the-world,* it's unlikely to carry the day—or the morning. Eventually, our commitment to a book will wane. A friend of mine was so committed to reading his Bible that he hit fourteen months straight without missing a day. He told me, "One day I made the intentional decision *not* to read, because the streak had become more important than my relationship with Jesus."

Spending time with a book—even THE BOOK—isn't what will cut it day to day. Your attitude, heart, mind, and soul must be convinced that each time you open the pages of the Bible, you're spending time with Jesus. The One who made you and knows you better than anyone. The One who created everything you can see and all that you can't. The One who died on the cross to pay the penalty for your sin. The One who is preparing a place for you in heaven and is coming again to receive those who have stayed faithful.

You're likely someone who has at one time or another genuinely tried to seek God through His Word. When you get up to seek God, are you finding Him? Let me assure you that if you're not finding God, it's not because He left. If someone moved, it was you.

Are you ready to break through the quiet-time ritual and get real with Him? He's never wanted your daily reading to just *look* spiritual. He's always wanted to get deeper and speak to you as your Lord, Savior, and friend.

The point of your quiet time is to connect with God. If you don't connect, you haven't maximized your time. God wants you to make every second with Him the best it can be. Besides your attitude about spending time with Him, there are many other factors that affect these most important minutes of your day.

Spotting Other QT Killers

Late nights. If you're constantly up late with friends or burning the midnight oil studying, it's going to be tough to wake up and give God your attention. Fatigue will make you think that God and/or the Bible is boring. Remember, He's your Creator and Redeemer. He doesn't deserve the worst minutes of your day; He deserves the best. Some late nights, of course, can't be avoided. But a good way to show God you're truly serious about hearing from Him is to make the conscious decision to get to bed early so you're not a zombie when you wake up.

I remember when I first did this. At first, I thought the alarm clock sounded like a demon. I'm certain I woke up delirious. But I forced myself to get up and seek God. I made a commitment that no matter how late I stayed up the night before, I would still get up and meet with God. If I got tired later in the day, that would be too bad. I would just have to learn to go to bed earlier. I have missed less than ten days in the nearly twenty years since I made that commitment.

Is it OK to spend time with God during other times of the day, like after school or before bed? The answer is . . . absolutely! God will take any time of the day you give Him. Ideally, however, He'd love to spend time with you as you *start* your day. That's when you need Him the most, before the day gets going.

Ignorance. Now I'm not saying you're ignorant, but some people haven't ever been taught how to spend time with Jesus by reading the Bible. They're ignorant as to how to hear from God. They think they have to read either ten chapters a day or nothing. The truth is, one good verse a day may be exactly what God wants to teach you. Other Christian students get the most from their Bible by reading large portions of Scripture and getting awed by the big picture of God's plan.

Though I'd suggest you get an appointment or two with your parent or youth leader so he or she can show you how to hear from God through the Word, here are a couple of tips:

- ◎ Say a prayer before you start and let God know you're wanting to hear His voice and get a word from Him for the day.
- ◎ Read the proverb (in the Old Testament) that corresponds with the day of the month. There are thirty-one proverbs, so you'll always have one to read.
- ◎ Read portions from Matthew, Mark, Luke, or John (known as the "Gospels") in the New Testament. They are four different accounts of the life of Jesus written by four men writing to four different audiences.

Not a Habit. The best way to build a consistent discipline of spending time with Jesus is to do it between two things you do every day. I know a lot of teens who take ten or fifteen minutes between taking a shower and eating breakfast. Others do it the moment they get up, before they take a shower. Still others get up early enough to shower and eat then have a quiet time before they catch the bus or drive to school.

The point is to find two things you do every day and build God into that schedule.

Poor diet. Did you know that your brain, muscles, and concentration are all affected by your diet? I'm no dietician, but I do know that if you're not eating healthy foods, your mind and body will be more fatigued. When you're fatigued, you don't do things unless you absolutely have to do them. And since spending time with Jesus could be viewed as an "optional" activity (optional in the eyes of the world), then these minutes are sometimes the first sacrificed on the altar of soda and potato chips. Start eating better and you'll have more than enough energy to hear from the Lord.

If you want to live God loud, you must carefully examine how you're feeding and exercising the temple of the Holy Spirit that God has entrusted to you.

Not a reader. Some people either didn't learn to read very well while they were young, are dyslexic, or have some degree of ADD (Attention Deficit Disorder). And now that they're teenagers, the thought of reading to try to connect with an invisible God is about as much fun as a trip to the dentist. While God sympathizes with this very real dilemma, there are alternatives. There are many versions of the Bible that can be bought on cassette tape. Find a version you like and take ten minutes or more a day to listen to God's Word. Another alternative is simply to read smaller portions of Scripture and when you find something new, write it down on an index card and carry it with you throughout the day. The key is to do what you can until you hear the message God has for you.

My experience has been that it only takes about twenty-four hours for your relationship with God to get stale. You have to do things that keep it alive or it will seem dry. Here are a few other specific things to keep your quiet times alive, and to keep you connected to God.

Examine Your Heart

It's difficult to approach God if you know your heart isn't totally clean before Him/ Christians have been given a wonderful gift: sensitivity to sin through the Holy Spirit. We don't have to wonder if something has come between ourselves and God. He is fully able to show us. Unconfessed sins are like bricks between us and God. The longer we fail to ask for forgiveness, the more bricks get piled up, until they seem to form a solid wall. It's tough to have a close relationship with someone who is on the other side of a brick wall! Honest confession and repentance immediately tears down that wall so that free-flowing communication can once again occur.

When you truly understand that God's nature is love, and that He's motivated by grace and not judgment, then you can start and end each day asking God important questions like:

◎ Is there anything in my mind that You're not proud of?
◎ Have I done or thought anything since the last time we met that has dishonored my relationship with You?
◎ Are there bricks that need to be removed between us before I try to hear from You?

Just ask Him to show you any area of your heart that is not pleasing to Him or is blocking your relationship with Him. Ask Him to reveal any sin you may have in your heart that He is hoping you'd repent from.

It is amazing how God will begin to speak to you when you ask these kinds of questions. Too many people sit in their quiet

45

times day in and day out never really hearing God's voice. He will open the windows of heaven and speak to you like a bolt of lightning if you sincerely want to hear. Once you have heard from Him on a thought or action that He wants you to get rid of, then go for it! Stand up like a man or woman of God and don't let anything get in the way of you becoming ALL God wants you to be.

After your sin is taken care of, you will begin to hear His voice in all kinds of other areas. You will hear His voice about your future. The Scriptures will come alive to you. You will have a clear line to the heart of God.

Choose to Worship Him No Matter How You Feel

I have discovered that to live God loud, I have to make a determination to worship God even when I do not feel like it. The truth is that no matter how I feel, He is still GOD! Whether I have a good day or not, He is still Creator of the universe. He is worthy to have all my heart—and voice—singing to Him with everything in me no matter how I feel.

The Bible says, "Enter his gates with thanksgiving and his courts with praise; give thanks to him and praise his name" (Psalm 100:4). If you want to get into God's presence, there is only one way to get there. You cannot beg or "just hope" to get in. You must worship your way in.

You must be determined to go for it. Do not be satisfied with having just a "pretty good time" with God. You have to go all the way. Sing to Him with all you have, even if you are the only one around. Grab some of the psalms and read them to God as if you wrote them yourself. Read them, or shout them, like they're coming from your heart! Say them until you mean them. You will be amazed at what will happen in your quiet times when you are determined to enter into real worship: God will show up and utterly convince you of His presence and power in your day.

Be Creative When You Are Reading Your Bible

What do I mean by being creative? Do not just sit down and read and then shut the book. Many people cannot remember what they read, even right after they read it. Here are some ideas to make your quiet times creative and to help you get some real meat out of God's Word:

Read through an entire book at once. Do not skip around from book to book. Ask yourself, "Who was God writing to? What did He really mean when He wrote it? What did the people He was writing to think it meant? There are many study Bibles that have an introduction to each book of the Bible. Be sure to read this; it will help you know a little more about why the person wrote the book. Then ask yourself, "What is God speaking to me today through this?"

Study the Bible by theme. Get a concordance (a book that lists all of the important words in the Bible by chapter and verse) and look up a word, finding where it is used in all different places in the Bible. For example, look up the word *forgive* and read all the different passages about forgiveness. God can completely change your life as you learn topic by topic about different issues you are interested in.

Read the same thing in the Word that a close friend is reading. For example, make a commitment to read through the New Testament together. As you are both reading through Matthew, write down questions you have about each chapter. When you get together, go over your questions and find the answers to help each other understand what God is saying. If there are questions you can't answer, bring them to a parent or a youth leader. Ask each other, "What did God teach you this morning?" See how God is speaking to both of you in different ways.

Read through a devotional book. While a devotional book should never be a substitute for reading the Bible, most are helpful guides. Find one that will help you understand more of the Word and apply it to your life. You could even get the same devotional book with a friend and work through it together. Just as before, ask each other what God is saying to you. There are many different devotional books available. You may want to use one that I wrote called *56 Days Ablaze*. (See my Web site address below and at the back of the book.)

Look for something new. When you read through the Gospels or even the Old Testament, look to see if you can discover more about God's personality in each chapter. Ask questions like, "Why did God say that?" or "Why did God do that?" Look for His character traits in every book of the Bible. Every single chapter will teach you more about how He does things. Since you are on a quest for more of God, sit down to read with the determination to discover more of who He is. Open the Word like a starving man would approach a banquet.

Write down one scripture from what you read each morning. Memorize it during the day. Take it with you everywhere you go. Chew on it all day long, just like chewing gum. Ask God how you can apply it to your life. There may be something He wants you to change today.

Log on. Log on to our Web site at http://www.acquirethe-fire.com and have your quiet time on-line every day. There are thousands of teens who are doing this, studying different themes each week.

Ask God for His Compassion for the People of the World

Do you really care for the people around you? Are you reaching out to them? What about the lost souls around the world? Do you care that they are lost?

It is time to be really honest with these questions. We know that we should care, but sometimes we still do not care.

I remember the day I suddenly woke up to the fact that I wasn't placed on this earth just to feel saved and to worship God. I grasped what true "lostness" is: total separation from God forever. I realized that if heaven and hell were real, I had to do my part to participate with God in reaching the world. He's the Savior, but I'm the instrument He chooses to use to bring lost souls to Him.

Are you having trouble understanding what "lost" really means? If so, share this feeling with the Lord. Be really honest with Him. The Bible says, "When he saw the crowds, he had compassion on them, because they were harassed and helpless, like sheep without a shepherd" (Matthew 9:36). Ask Jesus to fill your heart with the same compassion that He had.

The Bible also says that "God has poured out his love into our hearts by the Holy Spirit, whom he has given us" (Romans 5:5). Ask Him to let that love, which is already in you, be known in your head. Ask Him to let you see people through His eyes. Read about people from other countries and pray for them seriously. You might want to get a book called *Operation World* by Patrick Johnstone to help you pray specifically for people in other countries.[1]

Make a Commitment to Do It!

Now it is time to set an appointment time with God and keep it. Don't you dare let anything keep you from your time with

Him! This is more important than school, friends, or parties. It is more important than a movie or a meeting with the president of the United States. It is time you get to spend with GOD!

Set that time, then set your alarm and peel yourself out of bed! Splash cold water on your face. Tell yourself, "WAKE UP!" You have an appointment with the Creator of the universe!

When God sees that you are really serious about seeking Him, He will open up the windows of heaven. He wants to know you aren't just doing another Christian ritual. Keep it alive, keep it real, and stay honest with Him each day. Get serious about going after Him with all your heart every time you open the Bible. It is time to quit playing Christian games. Don't be someone who merely wants to look spiritual; be someone who is spiritual (and humble!) because you discover more of God each morning.

> ⏮ *When God sees that you are really serious about seeking Him, He will open up the windows of heaven.*

Live Loud
ACTION

If it's helpful, fill this form out:

I commit to getting up every morning like Jesus did (Mark 1:35) to meet with God and to seek Him with all my heart. I will read my Bible and pray during these times to grow more like Jesus each day.

Signed: _____

Date: _____

Live Loud
THOUGHT

"But Jesus often withdrew to lonely places and prayed" (Luke 5:16).

Section
TWO

◎ *Dating and Waiting*

The previous four chapters talked about having a passion for God, His Word, and His lordship. Without a knowledge and desire to live God loud, the words in the next four chapters will most likely ring hollow.

You and I were created to be passionate people. We have the built-in ability to focus all of our emotions and energy in one direction for good . . . or not so good. The passion God wants us to have for Him often gets . . . redirected, and I don't have to tell you where.

Let's admit the obvious: The opposite sex is mysterious and exciting. For many teens during the junior-high and high-school years, that excitement is as high as it will ever be. Believe it or not, God did that. He gave you the gift of passion for the opposite sex. But like any gift, it can be misused. And that's what has happened to countless Christian teens who genuinely want to live God loud. The result is that their hearts have been burned, their emotions have been crushed, and too many times their futures have been ruined.

One of the biggest pitfalls for teenagers and their walk with God is learning how to respond appropriately to their inner passions for the opposite sex. If you've ever been in a dating relationship, you know that it's tough to think about much of anything else. And if you're not in one, well, it's tough to think about much of anything else. The dilemma is that few know how to be a great Christian friend to someone of the opposite sex.

It's time to get serious about your walk with God and what He says about the boyfriend/girlfriend thing. God wants you to have a lifetime of success with the opposite sex, so naturally He wants you to *do things His way.*

I hope you didn't cringe while reading those last four words.

I know that you're heading toward adulthood. I also know that most teens want to do things *their* way. This is especially true in the whole arena of the opposite sex. As a young adult, you don't get to have too many things you can control, so you'd at least like to control this!

But the opposite sex is one area where you need to be "out of control." That is, God needs to have His say-so, not because He wants to ruin your life, but because He wants this important area to be the best it can possibly be.

I have talked to hundreds of young people who were doing great with God until they got into a dating relationship and became distracted. Like John. He got passionately committed to the Lord when he was sixteen. He was plugged into his youth group really strong, but then he began to date girls who were not Christians, "trying to reach them." He got trapped and tricked by the current dating system. He thought he "needed" a girlfriend. He ended up weeping bitterly after compromising his virtue by having sex with a girl. A gift he had at one time pledged to save for his future wife, he'd given away in a moment of passion.

The same mistakes are made even when teens date others in the youth group. Fortunately, John came back to the Lord and got his life right. Not everyone makes it back, and that is the real tragedy. Because there is *always* a way back.

You should know that the following chapters are not just a few nice ideas for you to think about. How you respond to the words in these next pages could determine your ability to live God loud during some of the most important years of your life.

Another thing you should know is that you won't find the answer to the most-asked question from Christian teens: "How far is OK to go?"

Why? I've discovered that trying to answer that question encourages the wrong mentality—that we should try to stay as close as we can to the gates of hell without falling in! I don't play that game in my life, and I would never encourage another Christian to do it.

We cannot take a Christian version of what the world is doing and think that it is God's best. God has different ideas, and His ideas relating to the opposite sex will save your heart from getting crushed, keep your body pure until marriage, and keep you fired up spiritually.

◄◄ *You should know that the following chapters are not just a few nice ideas for you to think about. How you respond to the words in these next pages could determine your ability to live God loud during some of the most important years of your life.*

Live God LOUD

Our world is plagued with the notion that everybody is fooling around before marriage. Every poll I read, however, even those from secular magazines, says exactly the opposite. Teens *think* everyone is doing it, but the fact is, there are just a lot of talkers who are too insecure to admit they're not doing it.

One area of the world that is doing it is Africa. Did you know that the entire continent of Africa is facing the fact that fully one-third of its population will die from AIDS in the next ten to fifteen years? The reason: They've believed the lie that abstinence until marriage is impossible. And it's not a "safe-sex" issue. Hundreds of thousands thought they would be protected by this practice, and yet the safe-sex line has failed to keep its promise.

In America, the way movies and TV programs depict sex outside of marriage, you feel like you're not normal if you wait. Hollywood glamorizes immorality, making it seem like anyone who wants to have any kind of real life has to fool around before he or she gets married. The entertainment industry only shows the "exciting" or passionate side of sex without showing the truth of what happens inside someone's heart when he or she gets involved sexually before marriage. I could tell you a thousand heartache stories, but you've already heard them.

God is looking for young people who love Him and want to live Him loud by standing up with pure lives dedicated to Him. No longer should you have to look down ashamedly as if you are embarrassed about being a virgin. There are a lot of great reasons to stay pure. But if you're still not convinced that waiting for sex until marriage is the way to go, let me share seven reasons why waiting is your best possible decision:

1. You could be dating your pastor's wife. When young people begin to date, few seem to take it seriously. They don't stop to consider whom the person they are dating might someday marry. I know a pastor who has his wife's high-school boyfriend in his congregation. He has said from the pulpit, "Someone here has kissed my wife!" That might sound kind of wild, but it's true. The person you date will be someone's wife or husband someday. Treat him or her like you would want your future spouse to be treated.

The Bible says in 1 Timothy 5:2 that we should treat the younger women in the church (your youth group) as "sisters, with absolute purity." Wouldn't you want to treat the young women in your youth group the same way you'd want a guy to treat your sister (with purity)?

Consider this fact: You and the sister in Christ in your youth group have the same Father. A Father who can see everything you do.

How would you feel if you had a daughter and you found out that someone was fooling around with her? What would you like to do to him? How do you think your heavenly Father feels when someone is fooling around with His daughter?

2. You can avoid the "date-'em-then-hate-'em" cycle. The teens I've known over the years from my years in high school until today do not know how to have a real friendship with someone of the opposite sex. When you do have a close friend, you usually say, "I know him too well to date him." Like anyone else, you'd like a few good friends who care about you. They want to date, though, because they think that dating will make a friendship stronger. When this doesn't work, they are fooled into believing, *The further physically I go with that person, the better friends we will be.*

Just the opposite is true. After a few dates, kissing tends to be the substitute of choice for real communication. Before long, kissing isn't quite as exciting, so more sexual involvement follows with the hope that it will make you closer. So, the all-too-common scenario on most weekends goes something like this: You go on a date looking forward to real companionship because you're lonely or bored or just really need to talk to someone. But soon, communication gets tough, so you start kissing and exploring. Instead of finding the companionship you were seeking, you end up substituting a racing pulse for true communication. While a racing pulse in the context of marriage is wonderful, when it's before marriage, it will leave you emptier than when you began. The very thing you want out of the relationship (a real friendship) is the very thing that physical involvement makes impossible!

As you make the commitment to avoid immorality before marriage, you will have a much greater possibility of having a real friendship with the person you date. Plus, you won't have any regrets when it's time to break up (and 98.5 percent of dating relationships in high school and college *do* break up). The closeness you really want is impossible to find if you get

> ◄◄ *The very thing you want out of the relationship (a real friendship) is the very thing that physical involvement makes impossible!*

involved sexually. The average relationship is completely sev-ered just three weeks after the couple has intercourse. Sex serves to enhance the closeness a couple has for each other only after they are married. It makes the relationship better because they chose to keep the order of things as God has planned it: friend-ship, love, marriage . . . then sex.

If you do not have a heart-to-heart friendship with a person, having sex will not give it to you. Getting physical before mar-riage only gives the relationship a false sense of closeness that isn't based on unconditional love. Sex before marriage truly is the destroyer of relationships. While it seems illogical to the world, it is the truth.

3. You could be looking for love in all the wrong places. Many young people think that if they could finally experience sexual intimacy, they would find real love. Countless young ladies have heard the words from guys, "If you love me, you'll let me . . ." In a desperate hope for someone who really cares, young girls have compromised their virtue. As a result, empti-ness and depression begin to hound a love-starved teen.

The love and acceptance you need and desire cannot be found in a passionate moment of immorality. True love respects á person's purity. A guy once asked me, "If it's really love, isn't it OK?" If it were real love, he would not even ask.

If sex equaled love, then prostitutes would be the happiest people in the world. As it turns out, they are some of the most miserable. Many times, teenage girls, looking for the love and acceptance they wish their fathers would give them, make des-perate attempts to get it from other guys. They come up feeling emptier every time.

4. You won't be able to look your sexual partner in the eye. The predictable question young ladies ask themselves after they lose their purity is, "Will he respect me tomorrow?" The answer is always NO! And worse still, you won't respect yourself, either.

Sex in the context of marriage is pure and holy and is nothing to be ashamed of. Genesis 2:25 says, "The man and his wife were both naked, and they felt no shame." Once Adam and Eve had sinned, the Bible says, they realized they were naked and sewed fig leaves together for clothes (see Genesis 3:7).

After giving away the precious gift of your purity in an immoral situation, there is only one way you can feel: ashamed. Many people feel ugly or dirty or like a dark cloud follows them around wherever they go. It is nothing to be proud of, even for guys. Yes, it's true . . . you have hormones, but so does the entire animal kingdom. God has made us qualitatively different from other mammals. We have the ability to say yes and no to our natural desires; animals don't.

I don't say this in a tough-guy way; I believe it with all of my heart: A real, godly man controls himself and treats young ladies with respect. And a real, godly woman treats herself with respect by letting her boyfriend know her limits *before* the situation goes too far.

Many Christian teens begin to see their entire walk with God erode because they become ashamed by how far they've gone sexually. It is amazing to think that a few moments of passion could make someone turn his or her back on God and miss the promised abundant life here on earth, or even the promised eternal life in heaven. But teenagers are taking that chance every day.

When I was a youth pastor, there was an eighteen-year-old girl in my youth group whom I'll call Jennifer. She knew the Lord, but she was very insecure. To compensate for her feelings of inferiority, she acted like the cutest thing God ever made. While she attempted to live and act like a Christian, she also had a seductive side to her. She had perfected a magazine-cover look in order to attract guys. While she thought it was all totally innocent, the guys around her were falling all over themselves to get her attention. Predictably, Jennifer got pregnant by a guy she had been dating (an older guy, because dating older guys is cool, right?) who did not even go to church, much less love the Lord.

After she found out she was going to have a baby, everything changed. Though she got up in front of the church and apologized, most who knew her could tell she was only sorry she got caught, not that she gave her virginity away. It wasn't too much later that she dropped out of youth group and eventually out of church. After she had the baby, she continued trying to get the attention of guys through her looks and actions. She has struggled with her walk with God ever since.

Having sex will *not* make you feel better about yourself.

5. It's a matter of life and death. We all know about sexually transmitted diseases (STDs), but nearly every teenager I've met thinks an STD could never happen to them. There are more than twenty-five STDs, and most are a lot more aggressive than you think. The facts are that 7,000 people die each year from STDs![1] Gonorrhea is contracted by 650,000 people each year and syphilis by 70,000.[2] Forty-five million people have chronic genital herpes.[3] Syphilis, passed through sexual intercourse or to the baby by birth, can be deadly if left untreated.[4] Five hundred thousand new cases of herpes, many strains being excruciatingly painful, are reported each year. Once infected with a herpes simplex virus, you're infected for life. There is no cure for herpes.[5] An estimated 900,000 Americans may be infected by the killer HIV/AIDS virus, which strikes an additional 45,000 people every year, about half through sexual contact.[6] Every year there are 77,000 new cases of hepatitis B due to sexual transmission, despite the availability of a preventive vaccine. Some cases end in cirrhosis or cancer of the liver.[7]

This all sounds pretty scary, and maybe even a little hopeless, but the good news is that no sexually transmitted disease can infect you if you follow God's plan and wait for sexual contact until marriage. A lifetime of regret can be avoided by one commitment of character.

The world—through public-school education, TV commercials, magazine articles, and scientific "studies"—will consistently try to convince you that as long as you practice "safe sex," you are "safe." The idea, of course, is to use condoms. The fact is that at least one out of every sixteen condoms is defective. This means that at least once every sixteen times you have sex, you are putting your life at risk. I think Christian teenagers are smarter than that.

6. It's worth the wait. God designed sex to be experienced only in the context of marriage. He knows that unconditional love within a lifelong commitment is the best way to get the most fulfillment and satisfaction out of this wonderful gift.

Remember, sex was God's idea! He invented it. He must know how it will be the best. Ultimate devotion to one person through marriage is a picture of how God wants our relationship with Him to be. God knows that to benefit fully from our relationship with Him, we can't have other gods clouding the picture. We must be wholly devoted to Him. Marriage is a picture of our undivided relationship with God. He wants us to have an awesome sex life, and He says the best is found when we're faithful to only one person our whole life. That's it. No regrets, no shame, only pure sexual intimacy the way it was designed to be experienced: in marriage!

There's an obvious truth that I hope you've picked up on. A high percentage of people—especially those famous and in the media spotlight—have already blown it. Their wealth and fame have convinced them that they are entitled to experience all things pleasurable whenever they want. It's natural to assume that they would then approve of you doing the same. Your immorality justifies their lifestyle. Most have no idea how great it would be if they married as a virgin. Have you ever wondered why anyone listens to what they say about sex anyway? If they're experts on sex, why don't they know the God who created it?

7. God said so. You have just read six common-sense reasons not to be sexually active before marriage. But just in case common sense does not make sense to you, here is the best reason: God says so.

In 1 Corinthians 6:19, Paul asks, "Do you not know that your body is a temple of the Holy Spirit, who is in you, whom you have received from God?" If you have given your life to Jesus, you have God living in you. You cannot take God's holy vessel (you) and put it in circumstances that consistently lead to sin. Just a verse back, in 6:18, Paul says to "flee from sexual immorality," and 1 Peter 2:11 says "to abstain from sinful desires."

Romans 13:14 tells us, "Rather, clothe yourselves with the Lord Jesus Christ, and do not think about how to gratify the desires of the sinful nature." This means we should do all in our power not to give it a chance to happen! While it's tempting and seemingly innocent, driving to a lonely place with your boyfriend (or girlfriend) only sets you up to fail. It sounds pretty simple, but if you just stay around a lot of other friends—and keep the lights on—you will stay pure.

If none of these other reasons has convinced you, stay pure because God says to. Even if you don't understand why. Just obey. One day you will be walking down the aisle of a church to get married. When you stand there looking your bride or bridegroom in the eyes with no shame, you will be glad you did things God's way.

I remember just after I became a Christian going on a date with a girl who went to a religious school. I was so excited that we could just go out and praise the Lord all night. However, I soon found out that she had other things in mind. When I took her home she literally began to attack me. While I wasn't exactly afraid for my life, I was for my purity. I stopped her and pushed her away long enough to ask, "Wouldn't you rather be reading the Bible right now?" She said, "No!" and kept attacking. I asked her again and she said, "NO!" I thought, *This is just great. All my life as a heathen I wanted this and it never happened! Now that I'm saved, it happens!* So I stopped her again and asked her the same question: "Are you sure you wouldn't rather be reading the Bible right now?"

She said, "No! Why? Would you?"

I replied, "Well, yeah, I would!"

She opened up her door and got out. She slammed the car door and stomped her way back to her front door.

Believe it or not, I drove away excited! *I said NO! I said NO! It felt so good to say NO!*

You can say no too.

One thing I learned is, DON'T PUT YOURSELF IN A POSITION WHERE THAT KIND OF THING WILL HAPPEN! It is a lot easier to say no when all the lights are on at McDonald's.

What If You Have Already Blown It?

"All this sounds great, but what if I've already messed up?"

There is good news for you. Jesus will always and forever . . . forgive! His love will wash away your past as if it had never happened. He will forget it, and He will help you to forget it too. You must ask Him to forgive you, and then you must repent. Put your foot down and say, "No more!"

Some people think, *Well, since I have already blown it, it doesn't matter if I keep messing up.* Wrong! The more you keep sinning, the more it will mess up your head, your heart, and your future marriage! It is time to stop, now. It is time to start over again. It is time to begin your second virginity.

That's right, I said second virginity! Now that you know

about living pure, you can stay pure from this time forward. You need to put some time between the present and the last time you messed up. The longer you stay clean, the more pure and holy you will feel!

The most important thing about being pure is your heart. God wants you to have what I call "the spirit of a virgin." Some people have never blown it physically, but they think about it all the time. They look at pornography or lust after other people. Their body might be pure, but their heart isn't. Those who get married with an impure heart are miserable. They do not have "the spirit of a virgin."

On the other hand there are others who have blown it big time. But they've repented, gotten their heart right, and kept their life pure. They've walked down the aisle without any shame because they knew they had "the spirit of a virgin," and now these people have great marriages.

Live Loud ACTION

Pray about, and then sign, the following sexual purity commitment:

SEXUAL PURITY COMMITMENT

Because my body is a temple of the Holy Spirit, I commit to stay free from any sexual activity, including petting as well as intercourse, until the day I get married. Thank You, Jesus, for the power to stay pure and holy every day.

Signed: _____

Date: _____

Live Loud
THOUGHT

"Marriage should be honored by all, and the marriage bed kept pure, for God will judge the adulterer and all the sexually immoral" (Hebrews 13:4).

Chapter 6 ◎ Should I Date a Non-Christian? The Myth of Missionary Dating

As you know, dating is an issue that nearly every teen has on his or her mind. And everyone seems to have their own opinions of what's right and what isn't. As a Christian, it's essential that you have your mind made up about what would please God in your dating life before you decide to date anyone. You can't live God loud by listening to your own counsel.

This is especially true as it relates to any consideration you may have had about dating someone who isn't a Christian.

I've known dozens of teens who've gotten into a romantic relationship with someone who isn't a Christian, thinking somehow God will use them to reach another. This reality proves that there are young people every day who are more committed to finding a boyfriend or girlfriend than they are to finding God on a daily basis. Some even think God sympathizes with the inevitable—dating a non-Christian—so that if they get into trouble, He will get them out.

I know a young lady who loves the Lord but is desperate to find a guy. She has been a Christian for years and has even been in leadership in her youth group. Everyone respects and looks up to her. For a long time she has been toying with the idea of dating a guy who's been wanting to go out with her. He is a new Christian and not very grounded in his faith. All her friends have talked to her and told her not to go out with him, but she refuses to listen. She says they are being judgmental because they do not really know him. Truthfully, she is using whatever excuse she can to keep thinking she is justified in dating him. The problem is, she wants a boyfriend more than she wants to do what is right. She could be in for some big trouble.

There are three major reasons why teens date and rationalize dating non-Christians.

1. It's the thing to do. In America, the seeking of "love" is glamorized above every other virtue. If you don't date, or you don't at least appear that you're trying to date, peer pressure makes you feel stupid and insecure. It's gotten to the point where even if you're only trying to be someone's friend, he or she will think you're really looking for romance. You get sucked into the subtle pressure that if you don't have a boyfriend or girlfriend, something must be wrong with you. For girls especially (but even for guys), their whole self-esteem sometimes revolves around whether they are going out with someone. As a result, a lot of time is spent trying to impress the opposite sex to lure them in your direction. "Dating equals happiness" is a lie far too many have fallen for.

This sad fact leads to an equally sad reaction from Christian teens: They feel "forced" to compromise their Christianity and end up dating anyone they can, even a non-Christian. If you have a lot of friends who are dating, and if your school's culture thinks it's cool and fun to date around, it might not be popular to continually stay solo.

There's another issue to deal with regarding dating: your personal happiness. You look around and see all the dating couples, and it *seems* like they are happy just because they're in a relationship. What no one seems willing to admit is if you are *not* happy before you date, you will *not* be happy when you start to date.

And if you're dating and unhappy, the next natural thought is, *Maybe it's because I need to get more intimate, or go all the way.* So you end up doing what you never intended to do just to be "happy."

Let me save you the trouble—find your happiness in a relationship with Jesus. He alone has promised to meet your every need by never leaving you or forsaking you.

You might not want to hear this, but if your reason for dating is you believe that you must have a "dating" relationship to be happy, then you're completely confused and shouldn't spend consistent time with the opposite sex. Wait to date. Let God show you that you are all right the way you are without a romantic relationship. Only then will you be mature enough to handle a relationship with the opposite sex.

2. For friendships and fun. Many young people date because they want companionship—someone to hang out with and have fun with. While these are valid desires and great benefits of a healthy relationship, are they good enough reasons to expose your heart and emotions to another who doesn't share your faith?

Don't underestimate the potential of a romantic relationship and the power it has to manipulate feelings and decisions. You may say, "It's not like I'm married; I'm just dating." But the fact is it doesn't take long for your whole life to begin revolving around one relationship. Emotions for the opposite sex are too powerful. That's why when a couple starts getting serious, most of their other friendships fall by the wayside. Add the false glue of physical contact as a substitute for communication, and you've got a recipe for a lot of years of regret.

If your reason for dating is for friendships and fun, go out with groups of friends and have a blast together. You don't have to expose your emotions to possible major damage (as you would surely do, especially if you are thinking about dating a non-Christian) just to have fun. Spend time with a bunch of "buds" whom you don't have to worry about impressing. Cut loose and enjoy being a teen without having to worry about getting your heart broken.

Fight the urge to get your emotions all tangled up with someone, especially a non-Christian, if what you really want is to just have a good time with friends. God can give you an amazing time with a crazy group of "live God louders"!

3. To find a potential partner. I'm sure you have heard that the Bible says, "Do not be yoked together with unbelievers. For what do righteousness and wickedness have in common? Or what fellowship can light have with darkness?" (2 Corinthians 6:14). This scripture is talking about friendships as well as romantic relationships. Definitely the most mature and wholesome dating relationships are between people who are serious about pursuing a lifelong mate. Whether or not you are dating someone to pursue a marriage relationship (and if you're still in high school, you're probably not), you need to seriously consider the truth of this passage.

Our maturity in Christ is measured by how obedient we are to the Scriptures even when it is not easy to obey. How committed are you to doing what is right no matter what this world or your friends say?

"But," you may say, "I am strong enough to date a non-Christian. I have been in church all my life! I am not a baby anymore."

The question is not, "Are you strong and mature enough to date a non-Christian?" The question really is, "Is any Christian strong enough?" Is it wise to put yourself in that position? When the devil tempted Jesus to go to the top of the temple and throw Himself down saying that God's angels would catch Him, Jesus said, "Do not put the Lord your God to the test" (Matthew 4:7). Getting involved romantically with a non-Christian is practically the same test. You are going against God's Word and then hoping He will pull you through if something goes wrong.

It's not a matter of whether your faith can endure it (for some, it can) or whether you can keep your salvation (you won't go to hell if you date an unbeliever). During your teenage years especially, you need to do everything you possibly can to mature as a Christian while not setting your faith up for a fall. You must live your Savior loud and passionately pursue Him with all you've got. You cannot afford to let anything slow you down or distract you. Dating an unbeliever, or someone who is not radically sold out to God, is definitely dead weight that will keep you from running the race unhindered.

To be yoked with someone means that you begin to get your hearts twined together. You begin to share special moments together and talk about deep issues. If you attempt this with an unbeliever, how can you share a common heart for Jesus? Is it possible to pursue any type of meaningful relationship if you look at life from completely different perspectives?

A fairly high percentage of Christians try to "missionary date" and bring their dates to the Lord. Though sometimes it works, most of the time it doesn't. I've just seen too many tragic endings to that story. Young Christians who want to live God loud wind up trashing their relationship with Him. They "fall in love" and forget about their "first love" (Revelation 2:4). They end up in a relationship, and sometimes even a marriage, that is lonely and not whole because God is not in the middle of it.

Sarah was another girl in my youth group who really loved the Lord. Her heart's desire was to someday be involved in ministry full-time with her husband. After dating several guys as a teen, she got more serious with one who seemed nice enough but did not have a *passionate heart* after God. He went to youth group, but it was clear he had no intentions of being in full-time ministry. She did not think much about it because, she told me, "This surely won't end up in marriage."

As time went on, they got more serious. He asked her to marry him. She was swept off her feet and forgot the lifelong dream of her heart, to be in the ministry. Right before the wedding we talked and she asked me what I thought. I told her I'd pray for her but that she would likely end up sorry because she was compromising her dreams. Her eyes told me she agreed, but she felt it was too close to the wedding to call it off (it's never too close if it is not right), so she went through with it.

> ◄◄ *This is not something to take lightly. The devil enjoys using a relationship with an unbeliever to totally mess up your relationship with the Lord. This is a matter of abundant life or spiritual death. Don't take a chance! Do it God's way. It is always the best.*

She told me later, "I knew within a week that I should have done what you said." Soon her husband got into pornography and wanted her to watch it with him. She went through years of pain and frustration, though she is finally serving the Lord as wholeheartedly as she can. She realizes that she will always live with the regret of missing her heart's desire and not being in the ministry full-time.

If you're thinking about dating a non-Christian, then know that the last thing non-Christians need is for you to date them. They need to be thinking about eternity and their relationship with God, not their feelings for you. You could actually keep them from having a relationship with God because they are infatuated with you instead of getting serious about God. If you really love them with God's love, stay out of their emotions until they have a sold-out, fired-up, turned-up relationship with the Father!

This is not something to take lightly. The devil enjoys using a relationship with an unbeliever to totally mess up your relationship with the Lord. This is a matter of abundant life or spiritual death. Don't take a chance! Do it God's way. It is always the best. He will totally blow you away with blessing if you stay committed to His Word and committed to pursuing a wholesome relationship with someone sold out to Him.

Live Loud ACTION

Write down the names of those of the opposite sex who aren't Christians whom you may be attracted to. Commit to pray weekly for their salvation, and NOT to go out with them even if they beg you to!

Live Loud THOUGHT

"Do not be yoked together with unbelievers. For what do righteousness and wickedness have in common? Or what fellowship can light have with darkness? What harmony is there between Christ and Belial? What does a believer have in common with an unbeliever?" (2 Corinthians 6:14–15).

Live God LOUD

Chapter 7 ◎ What Type of Love Affair Should I Be In? God's Dating Agenda

Having the desire to live God loud means you want to reach your full potential as a Christ follower. You don't want to settle for second, third, or fourth best—ever. The point I've been trying to make in the previous chapters is that teenage romantic involvement is where many a good life has been buried in the graveyard of unfulfilled potential.

Make no mistake: If you're going strong with God—especially as a teenager—Satan has one goal . . . to distract you long enough to pull you into something you can't get out of. And the method of distraction he uses most is our innate fascination with the opposite sex. For teenagers, that means dating. Let me quickly examine the reasons, good and bad, why most teens date:

◎ They find themselves in a short-term confusion, depression, or loneliness, so they get involved with someone they think will help.

> ◄◄ *Make no mistake: If you're going strong with God—especially as a teenager—Satan has one goal . . . to distract you long enough to pull you into something you can't get out of.*

- They want to find out what kind of person they should one day marry, what kind of man or woman of God they might best connect with.
- They are looking for security by attaching themselves to someone they think will unconditionally love and accept them.
- The opposite sex seems like the best of the alternatives.
- They want to play in the forbidden territory of sexual involvement.
- They're bored.
- The culture tells them they have to date.
- They want to experience real love.

One of the first commandments in the Bible is God saying, "Be fruitful and increase in number; fill the earth" (Genesis 1:28). You notice Adam and Eve did not disobey this command. Imagine Adam's face after God told him what He wanted them to do. I'm sure he didn't think, *Bummer, dude, but I guess I better obey the Lord!*

There are a couple of different types of love that you'll experience on your way to understanding what true love is all about. It's essential that you're able to identify these two loves.

Small-Time Love

Small-time love is what we're all most acquainted with. It's typically a fast and easy, counterfeit substitute for the real thing. You'll see it almost everywhere you look:

- all of the so-called love, sex, and dating on TV shows
- most of what you read in secular teen magazines and books
- junior-high and high-school relationships (most result in broken hearts at the very least, lost purity and unwanted pregnancies far too often)
- nearly all movies that have romance elements

Some small-time love in the media seems harmless because it's not advertised as the "ultimate true-love story." It's entertainment with a time limit, so it rarely can deliver big-time love. But while it has harmless elements, repeated viewing of movies or TV shows or constant reading of romance novels or secular magazines will train your mind to think small-time love is the best there is.

How do you start noticing the difference between small-time love and reality? You need to be brave enough to ask yourself some tough questions.

Here is a checklist to gauge your romantic relationships. If you've been in a dating relationship, check the boxes that apply.

When I'm in a steady dating relationship, I . . .

❑ think about the person I want to be with every thirty minutes or less.

❑ think about what my day and life would be like if we didn't have each other.

❑ think how devastated I'd be if we broke up.

❑ find it hard to pray and read our Bibles together.

❑ sometimes trade in my time with God for time with him or her.

❑ realize I had a more intimate walk with God before I started dating.

If several of these statements were true in your last (or in your current) relationship, you have likely bought into small-time love. Make the connection: If Meg Ryan and Tom Hanks can't stop thinking about their love life for two hours in a movie (*You've Got Mail* and *Sleepless in Seattle*), why should you be expected to do any different, right?

Wrong!

Love is wonderful and fabulous and awesome, and I hope everyone reading these pages finds the love that God has for them. But if it's small-time love, I fear you'll be on a path that will destroy your heart, life, and walk with God.

Big-Time Love

In the beginning, God made the earth, stars, plants, and sun; then He made all the animals. Everything He did was "good," the Bible says. Actually, everything He did was excellent, but something was missing. God had a dilemma. Now, hang with me here because I'm going to describe something about God's character that I hope sticks with you your entire life. If you get this, you'll get big-time love, and you'll realize the shallowness of small-time love.

The Bible says in 1 John 4:16, "God is love." He doesn't just have love; He is made of love. It's His nature. He loves without even thinking about it. It's all He knows how to be and all He wants to do. You can't get close to God without getting loved.

The problem is this: LOVE WANTS TO GIVE. God wanted someone to give to, someone to love who could really receive His love. He wanted someone who was built to handle His love and who could really enjoy it and appreciate it. None of the animals or plants were made of the right stuff to appreciate the awesomeness of His love. (Reread that last sentence if you need to.)

He wanted someone who could fully experience what it was like to really be loved by the Author of love, and who could reciprocate that love if he chose to.

So God decided He would make someone for the sole purpose of receiving His love. In order to make sure this new creation could fully appreciate His love, He said, "Let us make man in our image" (Genesis 1:26). In other words, in order for this new creation to understand love, Love (God) had to go back to Himself and make something out of Himself (Love) so that the new creation could receive and reciprocate His love.

Apparently, God made Adam and Eve for one reason: to be the object of His love. He made all of mankind so that all the power of His love could be aimed at us. You, therefore, are the object of His love. You've got a bull's-eye painted on you, and His love is the arrow.

Some have said we were created to have fellowship with God, or to glorify God, or to dominate the earth. But the original reason was that God had so much love He couldn't keep it to Himself. He had to give it, so He made you and me with the express purpose and ability to receive His love.

No wonder the Bible says things like:

- ◎ "Keep me as the apple of your eye; hide me in the shadow of your wings" (Psalm 17:8).
- ◎ "If I go up to the heavens, you are there; if I make my bed in the depths, you are there" (Psalm 139:8).
- ◎ "Neither height nor depth, nor anything else in all creation, will be able to separate us from the love of God that is in Christ Jesus our Lord" (Romans 8:39).

Here's kicker number one: *You can't really know love until you know God.* And remember, nothing you've done—no sin you think is unforgivable—can keep His love away. And it doesn't matter how fast you run, His love will run faster. You can't find a place where His love wouldn't go to get you. His love is in a relentless pursuit of YOU.

God has a love affair going on with you and the world, and He will not let go.

Here's kicker number two: *When you realize the purpose for which you were made (to be the recipient of God's love), you don't need a boyfriend or girlfriend to make you feel loved or important.* The Creator of love made you to love you.

When you truly understand the biblical truth that (go ahead, scream it out) "GOD LOVES ME!" nothing else comes close to being as important. You don't need someone like you thought you did. You need the real thing: the all-powerful, all-encompassing love . . . from God.

God Knows What You Need

Adam lived God loud by hanging out with Him. He just enjoyed getting blasted with His love every day. He was busy doing what God told him to do, naming the animals and tending to the garden (however boring we may think that would be, I'm sure to Adam it was pretty exciting). And he didn't have to look for a girlfriend or a wife. Remember, God is the One who said, "It is not good for the man to be alone. I will make a helper suitable for him" (Genesis 2:18).

In the same way, you don't have to hunt for love like other teens (and most adults) are doing. Adam was so blown away by being God's target for love, he didn't need or want anything else. The very first love affair was not between Adam and Eve; it was between Adam and God.

Ready for Some Real Love?

What does it mean to commit to a love affair with God?

It means staying away from dating long enough to really see things clearly. If you think you need a boyfriend or girlfriend, then you're not ready for a relationship.

Let your life become radically GOD-centered for an entire year (you read that right—an entire year), then let God bring you a person just like He did for Adam.

Date God for a year.

Until you've dated God for a year, you aren't ready to date anyone else. Let Him fill you with His love for a full year with no distractions.

Guys, commit to treat the ladies "as sisters, with absolute purity" (1 Timothy 5:2). Ladies, commit not to date, flirt with, or even hope for a guy for the next year.

The time you would have spent with your boyfriend or girl-friend, spend with God. Instead of taking time to pursue others, pursue God and pray. Instead of writing love notes, write in your journal what God has been doing in your life. Instead of thinking about someone else of the opposite sex, meditate on the Word. Instead of making plans to be with someone, make plans to live God loud!

You don't think it's possible? Read on.

I was on a Continental flight in a window seat when a young lady sat down next to me and we began to talk. I found out she was a Christian and had been living for the Lord for a long time. She was now in college and dating her first guy. Now let me be honest with you, this was not an ugly girl. I said, "Wait a minute. You are telling me that all through high school you never went on a date?"

She replied, "Nope."

"Why?"

She answered, "My dad wouldn't let me."

I probed a little deeper. "Did you have a boyfriend anyway, like at school? Or did you ever sneak out at night?"

"No."

I couldn't believe it! I asked her why her dad had that rule. She said that it started as a joke. "You are not going to date until you're twenty-five." The joke kept going on, and on, and on.

I asked her if she hated her dad. She said that she didn't and that this commitment had protected her from the multiple broken hearts she saw all her friends having to work through over and over. She went on, "I had a bunch of friends all through high school. The guys knew I couldn't date, so they would never ask me out. I had a group of guys who were my friends, some more like brothers. The girls knew I couldn't date, so they were never wondering if I would steal their boyfriends."

"Did you feel like you missed out on a lot in high school because you did not date?" I asked.

"I didn't. Every time a girlfriend of mine broke up with a guy, she would come crying to me with her broken heart. I never had to go through that."

At the time I talked to her, she was engaged to marry the first guy she had ever dated or kissed, and the joy on her face that she had saved her heart only for him was unlike any I had seen.

"Sure, that is great for the girls," you might be saying if you are a guy, "but what about us men? Real men have to date, don't they?"

I talked with a guy in Florida a few years ago at one of our Acquire the Fire events. He was a cool-looking guy who surfed a lot. He loved the Lord and was serving Him with all his heart. I asked him about his girlfriend. To which he replied, "I don't have one." I said, "Come on, I'm sure you have girls coming after you all the time. Why don't you date?"

He said that when he was thirteen he had made a commitment not to date. He remembered seeing a lot of his friends come to youth group and then start dating. "It seemed like every time they began dating, even if they were with someone who was a Christian, they started coming to church less and less. Every single person started falling away from God, and some have never come back."

Then he looked me in the eye and said, "I never wanted to take the chance of it happening to me!"

That is what I would call living God loud! That is big-time love . . . from God and for God!

I believe that God is looking for many more believers like these two young people who do not even want to take a chance of falling away from Him so have chosen to chill out on the dating scene.

Some of you have been looking for love from a boyfriend or girlfriend for a long time. Is it time to start getting your love from the Author of love? Is it time to experience big-time love and recognize small-time love for what it is?

Well, is it?

Live Loud Action

Take a week or more to pray, and perhaps even fast, asking the Lord to show you if you should not date for a year. Have your parents and youth leader pray as well. Then do what God is asking you to do. If you're convinced this is what God would have you do, fill out the certificate below.

Certificate of Courtship

I hereby commit my emotions, time, will, and body to seeking God and developing an intense love affair with Him for an entire year, starting on _____.

I will not seek to entice, flirt with, or lead anyone on. I will in no way initiate a romantic relationship with anyone. I don't need another person. I want to learn what it means to be in a true love affair with God.

Signed: _____

Date: _____

THOUGHT
Live Loud

"'Love the Lord your God with all your heart and with all your soul and with all your mind and with all your strength. . . . Love your neighbor as yourself.' There is no commandment greater than these" (Mark 12:30–31).

Live God LOUD

Chapter 8 ◎ *Do You Need to Dance?*
It's Time to Change Partners

I don't know whether I've made a strong enough case to you that the world's idea of romance doesn't measure up. If I haven't, well, I'm probably not going to earn any more points on the subject of dancing.

My heart and my goal in the previous chapters has been to encourage you to reach for God's best in your relationships with the opposite sex. I want you to search the Scriptures to get the full counsel of God so that you will never have to look back on your actions with regret. After hearing about the hundreds of broken hearts and shattered walks with God because teens chose to make the opposite sex a god, instead of worshiping the real God, it absolutely makes me want to cry and get mad at the same time.

So here's the question of the moment: "Is it OK to dance?"

My answer: Since I believe Christians should distance themselves from anything that even resembles the world's idea of romance (because it is "small time"), it is simply not a good idea. But far be it from me to ask someone to keep away from something without explaining why, so here goes.

The Attitudes

The word *dance* means "to move the body and feet to rhythm, ordinarily to music." The idea is that you move your body to the beat of whatever you are listening to. If you are listening to secular music, then you're moving your body as someone is expressing his ideas about life without God. I'll deal with the secular music issue in chapter 14, but I'm sure you see where I'm headed. You might say, "Does that mean we cannot even listen to secular music at a dance?"

Decisions, both good and bad, start in the brain and move their way to the heart. I'm convinced that the mind God created is an ultra-sophisticated supercomputer. That means that it can be programmed. And if you input garbage, that's what will come out.

If you're not interested in keeping your mind and heart pure, then I'll seem like a hardliner to you, but hang with me here for a few more paragraphs.

Say you go to a secular dance (a normal public-school dance or a teenage dance club). Not only are you getting what I'd consider garbage (music with lyrics that are nearly always anti-God) in your brain, you begin to move your body to it. You let the mood of a song that is talking about secular attitudes and lifestyles dictate how and when you will move your body. To me, this is a graphic form of letting the music tell you what to do.

Rave dances are the thing some teens are into lately. Not long ago, I went and watched teens at a rave club. The music was blasting with the seeming goal of trying to erase every thought in the dancer's head. The teens on the dance floor looked like they were dancing with themselves. Their eyes were shut, and they did not even know if their dance partner was still on the floor with them. It was like they were shutting out the rest of the world, trying to make their real life disappear, if only for a few minutes. I felt like these teens were simply a group of lonely

85

young people all hanging out together trying to lose themselves in the moment and forget the world.

The Overtones

Let's be real. Most of the time when you're with a dancing partner there are romantic or sexual overtones in the music and at the dances. The truth is that if you didn't come with a steady boyfriend or girlfriend, one of the side goals is to pick up on the opposite sex. Sometimes for the thrill of the hunt, sometimes for the thrill of what could happen *after* the dance.

You might say, "But that is not why I go. I just want to have fun."

I'm not so naive as to believe that 100 percent of the people who dance are doing it for the wrong reasons. There might be a percent or two who just like to dance (though they're probably not guys!). Some others like to flirt and act like they don't know they're doing it. After all, the game of getting the attention of someone, in essence leading him or her on to believe something that really isn't true, does have a thrill to it. Getting away with a lie is usually exciting enough to get your heart moving, right? (Be honest.)

Maybe you do not have bad motives, but you must admit, others do. If you're going to dances, you're exposing yourself to the unnecessary games and the risk of getting hurt by them.

The Bible speaks about dancing unto the Lord: "You turned my wailing into dancing" (Psalm 30:11). David danced before the ark of the covenant (see 2 Samuel 6:16). The idea here is that God's people were so excited they began to dance . . . to the Lord. If you are going to move your body in a wild, rhythmic way, it might as well be about something that is worth going crazy for.

There is a great example in the Book of Exodus of people getting really excited about the Lord. God had just parted the Red Sea, the Israelites had crossed through it, and a short time later all of Pharaoh's army had drowned. God had rescued His people again. It was a miracle! They were so psyched up they cranked up the tunes! (In other words, they sang and hit the tambourine, and possibly the drums.) They could not contain their excitement! They had to move their bodies. The Bible says that Miriam (Moses' sister) "took a tambourine in her hand, and all the women followed her, with tambourines and dancing" (Exodus 15:20). Why? They had a reason to dance.

The next time you see dancing in the Bible is when some of the same people were dancing in front of the golden calf they had made (see Exodus 32:6–19). They were not excited about the Lord anymore, so they made an idol. Sometimes I think Christians are the same way. They do not *feel* close to God anymore, so they find something else to get psyched up about. They find an idol to get happy about (secular music sings about a lot of modern-day idols). Then they move their body and dance to their idol—small-time romantic love—just like the Israelites did!

Moses saw what the Israelites were doing and got pretty steamed. In fact, he got so mad he threw down and broke the stone tablets of the Ten Commandments God had written out for him. I wonder if God has that attitude today with Christians who rejoice in things that have nothing to do with Him and everything to do with keeping their eyes in the wrong direction?

Dancing in Sync

Many young people in churches dance in sync to hip-hop tunes, gospel, and even island music. It's a worship routine that can really be quite amazing. As long as this is done to music with

Christian lyrics or instrumental music that is nonoffensive to the listener, it's a good thing and can even be a God thing. Most of the time these routines are performed as a ministry tool, so there is not even a hint of romantic or sensual suggestion.

"What about a Christian dance where Christian music is played?"

While the motive behind it may be good, and I've seen churches try to pull it off, it really is just a cheap imitation of what the world is doing. There is an appearance of godliness because the lyrics are good, but if everyone were honest about it, they'd say that the same attitudes of romantic and sensual enticement are present in the minds of the participants at "Christian dances" as at secular dances. I wish it were not true, but it is.

"But can't we teens who love God have any fun?"

NO!

Relax, I'm just kidding! Of course you can have fun, but if in your fun you're simply trying to imitate the world, then it shows that your minds have not really been transformed by the power of God. To live God loud you need to have a ripping blast with a bunch of fired-up friends like I described in the previous few chapters. Go out as a group. Experience an adventure together. But just do everything you can to make sure you're staying pure and holy. You do not have to imitate the world to have fun. God invented fun. So when you have fun God's way, you don't get the second-class thing; you get the real thing!

◄◄ *Of course you can have fun, but if in your fun you're simply trying to imitate the world, then it shows that your minds have not really been transformed by the power of God.*

ACTION
Live Loud

Make a decision about whether dancing—especially as the world does it—is something you think will move you further along in living God loud. This is either a yes or a no answer.

THOUGHT
Live Loud

"Finally, brothers, whatever is true, whatever is noble, whatever is right, whatever is pure, whatever is lovely, whatever is admirable—if anything is excellent or praiseworthy—think about such things" (Philippians 4:8).

Section THREE

◎ *Family Survival*

If you come from a stable, loving, two-parents-who-love-each-other-and-love-God family, you're absolutely in the minority. With the Christian marriage divorce rate overtaking the 50-percent divorce rate of non-Christian families (and yes, you heard me correctly), getting the encouragement from home that you need to live God loud is at an all-time minimum.

Jackie wanted to serve God with all of her heart after she became a Christian in high school. The youth group she was invited to had leaders who walked their talk—especially in their home. She was amazed at the love and commitment—and lack of tension—she'd see when she was invited over. She not only wanted that for herself, but she also wanted to be used by God to reach others who were just like her: lost in the world with only one hope of finding their way out. One minor problem: She didn't have a car and her parents wouldn't take her to church.

◀◀ *If you come from a stable, loving, two-parents-who-love-each-other-and-love-God family, you're absolutely in the minority.*

Sometimes this wasn't a problem. People from church would pick her up. But since she lived fifteen miles away, it wasn't always convenient to get a lift, especially if she wanted to go to Wednesday- or Sunday-night services.

Did Jackie's parents congratulate or encourage her in her new faith? Not a bit. In fact, her dad would constantly put Christians down. He laughed at her new beliefs and never once showed interest in her relationship with God. Mom was a bit softer, but she had abandoned God years before to get married to her husband. Her guilt kept her from doing much more than saying, "How was church today?"

Randy's parents were Christians . . . but just the Sunday variety. Church was a habit, as was table grace, but there was rarely a meaningful conversation about the Bible, Jesus, or how to live the Christian faith. Randy knew from his own experiences at camp and at church that God was much more real and dynamic than his parents were portraying, but he couldn't put *church* and *mediocrity* together. It didn't compute. He told me, "If God is really real, why doesn't everyone who's been going to church for twenty years have more excitement about the Lord?"

There are pockets of revival breaking out all over our nation among today's teenagers. It's one of the most exciting God-things I've seen in the last fifteen years. Many teens tell me how they want to live God loud but their mom and dad are either not saved or do not live what they preach. Disillusionment about the Christian life based on what teens are seeing and hearing at home has the power to quench the fires of revival and turn down the volume of God that teens like you are trying to turn up.

And what if both Mom and Dad are Christians . . . yet they are pursuing a divorce? Some teens have told me of intense circumstances in their homes involving a dysfunctional parent or a new stepparent. "How do I deal with my mom who is an alcoholic?" or "What should I do about my dad who is an elder but sexually abuses me?"

These next few chapters are designed to help you gain godly perspective on and genuine help for some of the most intense predicaments in the family I've seen.

As you read, do me a favor: No matter what your circumstances, please do not judge the goodness of God based only on what you see from your parents (especially if it's negative). He is bigger than that. Adults are sinners like everyone else. Sometimes they've learned to confess their sins and push ahead to become more like Christ; other times they're just better at hiding their sins. Whatever situation you are facing right now, I am confident that God will help you as He helped me get through some rough years with my folks.

> ◄◄ *No matter what your circumstances, please do not judge the goodness of God based only on what you see from your parents (especially if it's negative). He is bigger than that.*

Live God LOUD

**Chapter 9 ◎ How Do I Get More Freedom?
You Can Get Your Parents to Let
You Do Whatever You Want to
Do**

Are you the type of teenager who is constantly wishing for more freedom at home?

Sure you are.

The desire for more freedom is a good thing. But you've probably noticed that sometimes it turns into rebellion when you don't think you're getting your freedom quickly enough. When your parents see rebellion in you, they do the exact opposite of what you want them to do: They clamp down.

Do you want your parents to let you do what you want? I'm going to give you a key that will unlock the freedom door of your life.

You must HONOR them.

"Why Honor Them?"

Answer: *It's been God's plan from the beginning.*

God created Adam and Eve and told them to "rule over the fish of the sea and the birds of the air and over every living creature that moves on the ground" (Genesis 1:28b). Though it doesn't say specifically, this verse also includes ruling over their children. God put the parents, not the kids, in charge of the family.

You may not like hearing this, but in most homes—even Christian homes—disharmony and problems can usually be traced to the fact that the kids are running the house. They boss their parents around or manipulate them, and to avoid conflict, the parents cave in. When this happens, the order of how things should be run gets reversed. The results are confusion and tension.

Let's say, for example, that Susie asks her mom if she can go to the football game on Friday night. Mom says, "No, you got an F on your history test this week. You need to stay home and study."

So Susie goes and asks Dad, and he says, "You are my little girl. Of course you can go."

Mom walks by Susie's room on Friday night as she gets ready to go and says, "I thought I told you that you couldn't go." Susie responds, "Dad said I could." Mom goes to talk to Dad about it, and a fight explodes as Susie is walking out the door.

What are other ways you and your friends try to manipulate Mom and Dad? Whining, crying, threatening, being openly rebellious, isolating yourself from them, and rolling your eyes are just a few. I'm not dumb enough to believe that all the tension in a home is created by teenagers. But most blowups can be avoided by treating your parents with respect.

Romans 13:1–2 says, "Everyone must submit himself to the governing authorities, for there is no authority except that

⏮ *In most homes—even Christian homes—disharmony and problems can usually be traced to the fact that the kids are running the house.*

which God has established. The authorities that exist have been established by God. Consequently, he who rebels against the authority is rebelling against what God has instituted, and those who do so will bring judgment on themselves."

If you've ever wondered why things don't seem to be going right in your life, check to see if you are bringing judgment on yourself by not honoring your parents.

When Adam and Eve were the king and queen over the earth, they were charged with raising princes and princesses who would:

◎ be responsible
◎ be smart
◎ know how to think
◎ be sober
◎ be obedient to God
◎ make wise decisions
◎ be able to govern and lead others
◎ have a broad perspective on life

Your parents have the same mandate: to raise you as a prince or princess, ready to govern skillfully when you are of age. God gave them this responsibility. That is why it is so important to honor them.

"What Are the Advantages of Honoring My Parents?"

Answer: *Plenty!*

Ephesians 6:2–3 says, "'Honor your father and mother'— which is the first commandment with a promise—'that it may go well with you and that you may enjoy long life on the earth.' "

God promises that if you honor your parents, He will blow you away by blessing your life for a long, long time. The blessing and favor of the Lord are on your side when you honor your parents. You can be sure you are on the right track to fulfilling all your potential if you stay submissive to the authority that God gave your parents.

"How Do I Honor My Parents?"

Answer: *Honor your parents by listening to them.*

Proverbs 1:5 says, "Let the wise listen and add to their learning, and let the discerning get guidance." Do you really want to be smart? Then listen to Mom and Dad. I know it's a novel concept, but just try it. It's amazing how many mistakes it will keep you from making. Don't just do it because you're supposed to; do it to really find out why their instincts and knowledge are saying go this direction, when yours are saying go that direction. Ask them questions so you can get their perspective. Ask "Why?" a lot, but not with an attitude. Get their views of why they have particular rules for you, or why they don't want you to do something. Communicate to your parents that when you are trying to find out the reasons for their rules, you're simply trying to understand their perspective. It will help them think through their rules (and probably loosen up on some rules that shouldn't be there).

But you have to do all your questioning with a tone of respect that communicates honor. As you learn from your parents by listening to them, the things you think you should be doing to have more freedom just might change because you've become smarter.

◄◄ God promises that if you honor your parents, He will blow you away by blessing your life for a long, long time.

"How Else Can I Honor Them?"

Answer: *Three ways.*

1. Honor your parents in the way you speak to them. So many teens bring shame on themselves by the way they talk to or about their parents. The Bible says in Ephesians 4:29, "Do not let any unwholesome talk come out of your mouths, but only what is helpful for building others up according to their needs, that it may benefit those who listen." This is hardly the case between teens and parents. If you're murmuring under your breath after they tell you to do something, or you have volcano anger when they exasperate you, it's past time to think before speaking.

I remember when I was sixteen and my dad and I got into a fight about my car. I wanted to take it, and he said no. He had my keys in his pocket. I said, "Give me those keys, or I will tackle you and do whatever I have to do to get them." I was a little bigger than my dad at the time, so he gave me the keys. And even though I have since apologized, I have regretted those words and that confrontation for a lot of years. Instead of respecting the authority God had given me in my dad, I humiliated him.

Did you know that parents have feelings too? Many parents have been deeply hurt by the things their kids have said to them. Even if your parents aren't (in your opinion) doing the best job in the world, they brought you into this world and they are more than likely doing their best to raise you right. (It should be mentioned that there are some parents who weren't raised right themselves and don't have a clue how to raise you. But they are the exception, not the rule.)

An overwhelming majority of teens say they occasionally or consistently lie to their parents. *Is this honoring them?* Honor your parents by always speaking the truth. While the short-term consequences may not be fun (especially if you've messed up), the long-term fruit of them being able to trust in your word will give you more freedom than any one hundred lies could ever do. Freedom comes through trust. Trust through honesty. Honesty is easier when you have the attitude of honor in the forefront of your mind.

2. Honor your parents by obeying them. Ephesians 6:1 says, "Children, obey your parents in the Lord, for this is right." I know obedience sounds more like slavery than a vacation. But this is God's way of doing things because He knows it's the best way.

Colossians 3:22 says, "Slaves, obey your earthly masters in everything; and do it, not only when their eye is on you and to win their favor, but with sincerity of heart and reverence for the Lord."

Do you want to give your parents a shock? Then bend over backward to obey them. Not just their commands, but their desires as well. Don't try to just slide past them with minimal obedience. That will only get you minimal freedom. And quit trying to get away with all that you can. Parents know way more about you than you think they do. They've been living with you for thirteen to eighteen years, so they can read you like a book.

Find out what they really want done, and do it. Go for the spirit of the law and not just the letter of the law. You will absolutely blow them away if you do what they want. Obey your parents even when you don't agree with them—especially when you don't want to. That's your chance to prove you are submitting to their God-given authority, and this pleases the Lord.

The more willingly you submit and obey from your heart, the more open your parents will be to letting you have more freedom.

3. Honor your parents by showing responsibility. Many teens want the opportunity to make their own decisions but have not really shown they are responsible enough to do so. Jesus told the parable of the talents in Matthew 25:14–30. The master commended his servants, saying, "You have been faithful with a few things; I will put you in charge of many things" (v. 21). If you want to have more responsibility, you must show that you are awesome at handling the little you have now.

How do you spend your free time? How about your money? How fast do you drive? Any traffic tickets? These are all obnoxious neon signs that communicate to your mom and dad exactly how responsible you really are. If you don't prove faithful in the small things, they will never give you more freedom.

Do you want to give your dad a head-scratching fit? Don't always try to take a free ride. Try to pay for your own stuff once in a while instead of asking him for money all the time.

Do you want to make your mom pass out? When you are in the wrong, admit it. Confess your mistakes and ask her to forgive you. When you do this, you are taking responsibility for your actions. And remember what responsibility leads to? That's right: freedom.

I remember doing something wrong on purpose not long after I became a Christian. I did it just so I could admit it, show my parents I was responsible, then take my punishment. My dad never said anything to me about it. Two days later I asked, "Dad, did you know I was out all night a couple of nights ago?"

He said, "Yes."

I said, "Dad, did you know that the Bible says that a man who doesn't discipline his son hates his son? Dad, do you hate me? And what about the verse that says, 'He who spares the rod hates his son, but he who loves him is careful to discipline him' " (Proverbs 13:24).

He simply responded, "I think you're starting to grow up, Son."

The Dangerous Turn

It's good to desire more freedom through responsibility, but don't let your desire for it turn into rebellion. If you start thinking, *I'm old enough; I'm gonna do it anyway*, you immediately get OUT OF GOD'S BLESSING. When that happens, get ready for your life to get really messed up.

As you prove your responsibility and honor your parents, God will open doors in your life you will not believe! Nearly every good thing that happens to you will be because you've honored God or honored others. Being someone who has learned the secret of honoring will make you go far in life in any endeavor you try.

Live Loud ACTION

Stop right now and take some time to ask God to forgive you for any way you may have dishonored your parents. Think of each specific situation where you were disrespectful to them, and ask God to forgive you. Make a commitment to God to honor your parents with all your heart. You may even want to go and talk to your parents about it. Ask them to forgive you. It does not matter if they have made a mistake; do not expect them to ask you to forgive them. You do it first. You will be amazed at what will happen in your relationship with your parents when you begin to honor them.

Live Loud THOUGHT

"Honor your father and your mother, so that you may live long in the land the LORD your God is giving you" (Exodus 20:12).

Live God LOUD

Chapter 10 ◎ What Do I Do If My Parents Don't Really Know God? Dealing with Pre-Christian or Nominal-Christian Parents

As I travel all over North America speaking to thousands of teenagers each week, the most heartbreaking stories I hear are how poorly many Christian young people are being treated by their parents.

Some have parents who call themselves Christians—but you'd never know it if you looked at how they treat their kids. Others have parents who are not Christians—and they subject their believing son or daughter to daily persecution and intimidation.

I talked to one teenage guy a few years ago who was crying his eyes out trying to forgive his mom. He asked me what he should do about her because she was constantly drunk. Though he wanted to follow the Lord, she was making it really hard for him even to survive.

Another guy used to get drunk and in trouble with the law every weekend, and his parents did nothing but tolerate his behavior. "Boys will be boys." But as he got turned on to the Lord, they started harassing and making fun of him. My own father did that to me as a teen. I found out through a third party that he was calling me a "Jesus freak" and acting like I had gone off the deep end after I got saved.

Why do parents do this?

Some may think their kid has actually joined a cult. Others feel guilty because their child wants to live a more pure life than they did or are doing right now.

I talked to one girl who went on a mission trip with Teen Mania Ministries a few years ago. While she was gone, her parents decided to surprise her. They stood in line at 4:00 A.M. to buy her tickets to a secular hard rock concert that was coming to town. When she returned and they told her about the tickets, she told them she didn't want to go because she didn't want that kind of influence in her life anymore. They went ballistic! They were furious that she "loved God" too much to go. They didn't look at the maturity of her stand; they only looked at their inconvenience. And her parents were churchgoers!

My purpose is not to judge whether some parents are Christians or not, because only God can judge a heart. While some will openly admit they are not, others claim they are believers. No matter what they are, it's important to know how to respond to them whatever the circumstances may be, because a teen's response to his or her parents should always be consistent.

Why Obey?

All parents who have read the Bible have one favorite verse, and they are usually careful to make sure their child learns it. It is one I mentioned in the last chapter: "Children, obey your parents in the Lord, for this is right. 'Honor your father and mother' " (Ephesians 6:1–2).

It's weird, but even parents who do not know anything about the Bible seem to know this verse, and they love to use it to try to convince their kids to honor and obey.

Let's examine this passage a little more closely. It says children are to obey their parents. The word *parent* means "to produce."

When you *parent* something, your goal is to produce something that will be strong and healthy, like a gardener parents his garden. You tend it until it produces a healthy crop. In order to do that, you must water the plants and fertilize the soil.

That is exactly what parents must do to help their teens grow up to be mature and wise. Parents must water and fertilize. They should be pouring into you the ingredients you need to succeed in life. Sometimes they even have to pull a few weeds that crop up in your life (i.e., not let you do the things that may be counterproductive to your life). The Bible implies that when God gives to you these people who are pouring into your life, you should obey them with all your heart. Why? They are looking out for your best interests. Does this mean we should blindly obey every whim of our parents, even if what they want us to do isn't scriptural? Let's talk about the concept of honoring again.

Honoring When It's Hard

You may be in a situation in which it is extremely difficult to honor your mom and dad. Honoring is different from obeying. As an example, let's take out the garbage.

When you take out the garbage because Mom told you to, it does not mean you honored her. If you did it with a bad attitude, there was no honor. Some teens think that if their parents are really mean to them, they do not have to honor them. The truth is, honoring your parents has nothing to do with the way *they* treat *you.*

You honor your parents because of their position, not because of what they have done, good or bad. We honor the president because of his position. You might not like his policies, his philosophy, or the way he does his hair. But he is the president of the United States, and you honor him because of that.

The same principle is true regarding your parents. You may

not like their rules, their philosophies, or the clothes they wear, but they are your parents. God gave them that position. Of all the people in the world, He chose those two to bring you into the world. No one can take that position away from them. No matter what bad or good things they have done, God made them your parents. Consequently, He wants you to honor them.

So, what is the difference between honoring and obeying? If your parents asked you to do something illegal or immoral, it would not bring them honor for you to follow through on what they asked. If people found out, they would think, *What terrible parents you must have to raise you like this.* God gave you a conscience for a reason. He wants you to follow what you know is right. If I would have "obeyed" my parents' wish about my college choice, I never would have moved away and gone to a quality (and expensive) Christian college. Of course, now people look at me and say, "What great parents you had!" The truth is, neither one of them was a Christian, and both would have preferred that I stay near home and go to a secular school. If I had "obeyed" their preference, I would not have brought them honor like I do now.

"Does this mean that whenever I want, I can selectively obey my parents?" Not at all! *"Does it mean that if my parents are not Christians, I don't have to obey them?"* No way! Most of the disagreements that teens have with their parents have nothing to do with whether something is scriptural or not. It has to do with whether they would prefer to do a chore or not.

The general rule would be to obey your parents no matter what. If indeed you think you have a biblical reason not to obey (what they are asking is blatantly against the Bible), then you need to talk to your pastor, youth pastor, or others in leadership before you make any drastic moves. They may be able to help you talk to your parents. Find out why your parents want you to do what they are asking. See how you can obey the spirit of their rules if not the letter. The point is, you want to have other people backing you up so that you are not all alone, going against your parents' wishes just because you want to bag out on one of their orders and be rebellious.

Verbal Abuse

Maybe you are in a situation where you are constantly being ripped to shreds by what your parents say. Unfortunately, there are parents who say things that just cut the heart right out of their teen, and sometimes they do not even realize what they are doing.

Many times, even parents who say they are following the Lord end up saying things that totally tear at the self-esteem of a young person. Teen Mania has done surveys of thousands of teens and found that the things they have been most discouraged by have often come from parents. It is easy to feel completely paralyzed and demoralized if a parent is saying hurtful things to you.

I remember thinking when I was growing up that I'd probably never make it in life. I thought, *If my parents are saying these things to me, and they are supposed to love me the most, I guess I really am a loser.* I felt the pain of words I heard from them that cut my sense of self-worth down to nothing. I felt worthless. I even remember wanting to end my own life after hearing hurtful things my parents said to me.

If you are right in the middle of a situation like this, you need to remember that you have a heavenly Father. He only speaks words to you that lift you up (see chapter 13). He is there to give you the truth even when you think no one else will. He knows exactly how low you feel and the pain that is inside. For those going through parental verbal abuse, I know it will seem almost impossible for you to hang on, but you have a lifeline to reach out to, so use Him. Escape with your Bible, and let your Father in heaven pick you back up and help you carry on.

Distant Fathers

There are many teens who feel very distant from their fathers. Though they live in the same house, they might as well be living in another city for all of the attention they get from him. Obviously, if your parents divorce and your father moves out, you are going to feel even further away from him. And this only increases if you never hear from him or if he remarries. If your mom remarries, then your father feels strange coming around with the new man there, or he feels like you have a live-in father figure now and don't need him as much anymore.

Most teens, however, still have two parents living at home. Yet some dads have been known to spend so much time reading the paper or watching sports that they never really talk. It's easy in these circumstances to think there is something wrong with you. Nothing is further from the truth. Some men are just absolutely clueless how to communicate with their children.

I have prayed with hundreds of young men who wish that they had a godly father in their life. Each week as I speak at Acquire the Fire conventions, I see hundreds of teenage guys crying their eyes out because their dad has let them down. They feel like they do not even know their own father. Most guys won't get mushy and say, "I wish my dad would say 'I love you' to me," but this really is the heart of the matter. It is absolutely the most normal thing in the world to want that in your life.

I have also talked to many teenage girls who wish they were close to their dad. As a result of his absence (emotional or physical), they will sometimes desperately seek attention from other males. And it's rarely the right type of attention they end up with. Many teenage girls dress in whatever it takes in order to catch the eye of a guy. When they've caught one, they'll do what they must—even to the point of giving away their purity and dignity—to keep him or to get him to "love" them.

I talked to one young lady who was just getting ready to graduate from high school. She had invited her dad, who had divorced her mom when she was little, to the ceremony. Though she had not seen him in about ten years, he came. A few months later, she talked with him on the phone and was just making small talk, telling him what was going on in her life, when he said, "I am so proud of you."

The girl couldn't speak and began to cry on the phone. "Dad, I have waited eighteen years to hear those words come out of your mouth."

It is never God's plan for a girl to wait that long to get affirmation from her dad! If you are a teenage girl trying to get a guy's attention because you don't have a strong father figure in your life, let me tell you something: The type of love a teenage guy is able to give you is most likely worse than "better than nothing." You don't need that kind of love. What you need is the kind of acceptance that only a loving father can give you. You will NEVER find it in a cute guy, and you're sure never going to get it by giving yourself to him. If you cannot get it from an earthly father, then you have a heavenly Father ready to wrap His arms around you through the power and grace of His Holy Spirit. He is able to do this by sending others into your life and by giving you an extra measure of truth through His Word. If you seek Him, you will find Him. In fact, whether you are a guy or a girl, God says He will be "a father to the fatherless" (Psalm 68:5).

So if your father is gone out of your life, or if he lives at home but you feel far away from him, God will be your Father. He promised He would. You just need to call out to Him and ask Him to be a Father to you. I know it sounds trite, even a little cheesy, but if you need a father, the truth is that God is there for you.

Other Injustices

In a world rampant with families falling apart, it is becoming more and more apparent that the young people of today have been given the short end of the stick. An injustice, according to the dictionary, is a violation of a person's rights. You have a right as a member of the human race to have two parents in your home. It is not asking or hoping for too much to desire a stable home life.

Some young people have a parent who is an alcoholic. Naturally, kids don't come with instructions on what to do about *this* dilemma. I have talked to some teens whose parent has a live-in boyfriend or girlfriend. Others have been physically abused by their parent's live-in or even by their own parent.

Some even have parents who will use their Christianity against them every time they make a mistake. They'll say, "I thought you were a Christian!" While Christians can't be perfect, that's the way some view us. They think that because we believe in Jesus as our Savior, we are suddenly as perfect as He was. While it's our goal to be more like Him, our imperfection is the reason we need a Savior in the first place! When a parent starts using that line, there's not much you can do. As I said earlier, some will mock your commitment to Jesus, while others will punish you by not letting you go to church or youth group because they know you like it so much.

I want to let you know that in spite of all these obstacles, you can overcome! Your parents are not the enemy; the prince of darkness is.

It is time to live God loud no matter what your situation may be. While I don't want to downplay the intensity of the situation you may be in right now, you must believe that Jesus knows exactly what you are going through. He will meet you in the quietness of your own heart and give you the grace and power to be strong!

Finding Christian "Parents"

As I said earlier in this chapter, a parent is someone who nurtures and helps you grow and mature. If your parents are not Christians, God is able to give you surrogate Christian parents (substitutes without taking away your own parents) if you ask Him. While you keep praying for your parents' salvation, these people can provide the role models and godly advice you need to become a man or woman of God. You just need to ask God to provide, then begin looking for them among the people at your church. Ask your pastor or youth pastor to help.

Remember this: While you are looking, or even when you find them, you do not have an excuse to be openly rebellious to your biological parents. Do not use your Christianity as an excuse not to obey. Do not EVER say, "Well, you are not a Christian. I don't have to obey you." Or, "I can do what I want since you are not saved anyway." Whatever you do, you want to be an example to your parents of what a good Christian is really like.

Jesus said, "Let your light shine before men, that they may see your good deeds and praise your Father in heaven" (Matthew 5:16). Let your parents see the living God in your life. Keep turning up the volume of Him with all your heart. If you are facing tough times at home, tell your leadership at church so they can pray with you about it. Don't try to "buck up" and think you can navigate intense situations all by yourself. God wants to help you in a big way to make it through your teen years.

Live Loud
ACTION

Whether your parents or stepparents are Christians or not, take a thirty-day challenge to pray for them. There are always a lot of people praying for you, but what about for your folks? Don't they need prayer too? For thirty consecutive days, commit to pray earnestly that God would make Himself real in their lives; that their jobs would go well and that they'd find fulfillment in what they do; that they would become more like Jesus; that they could live at peace with other adults around them; and that they would be the parents you need to live God loud.

Live Loud
THOUGHT

"But mark this: There will be terrible times in the last days. People will be lovers of themselves, lovers of money, boastful, proud, abusive, *disobedient to their parents,* ungrateful, unholy, without love, unforgiving, slanderous, without self-control, brutal, not lovers of the good, treacherous, rash, conceited, lovers of pleasure rather than lovers of God—having a form of godliness but denying its power. Have nothing to do with them" (2 Timothy 3:1–5, italics added).

Live God LOUD

Chapter 11 ◎ What If My Family Doesn't Come with Two Originals? Divorced Parents, Single Parents, and Stepparents

Divorce happens so often that it's easy to conclude that it's a normal part of life. When I was a kid, it was very abnormal, even embarrassing, if your parents were divorced. Now it's no big deal.

Society likes to tell us that there are just different kinds of families. Some have only a mom, others a dad. Some have a stepparent, and others live with people who are not their parents at all (such as other relatives or foster parents).

When a divorce does happen, I've seen a lot of teens try to act like it doesn't bother them. "It's a fact of life, so why should it upset me? And, even if it did, what would I do about it? So what? My parents got a divorce. Who cares if I feel ripped off in the middle of the whole thing?"

God cares.

The Bible is clear when it says that God hates divorce (see Malachi 2:10–16). It is because divorce was never a part of His original plan for marriages, and He knows how much it hurts children when a father and mother split. God never intended for marriages to end. Jesus said, "Therefore what God has joined together, let man not separate" (Matthew 19:6). So, if your family has gone through a divorce and your heart and head are confused about it, don't feel like you are the one who has the problem. We will talk about how to get over the impact of a divorce in the next chapter (dealing with forgiveness).

If your home doesn't come with two originals, how should you live day by day, given your parents' situation? If your mom and dad are still single, or if one of them is seeing someone, what should you do? What if they get remarried? How should you deal with the stepparent?

These are complex questions, and we must look to the Bible to find God's way of handling them.

The Single-Parent Family

When a family separates after a divorce, many of the same dynamics apply as if a person has died. The sense of loss the mother feels, if the father left, is similar to that felt by a woman who has just become a widow. The emptiness she feels after part of her life has been torn away and her heart ripped out is only worsened by the fact that it did not happen through an accident or physical disease.

The loss that young people feel at their parents' divorce is similar to what orphans feel at the loss of their parents. They are bereaved or, in other words, deprived of the love and constant relationship with the person who has left the home. They feel stripped and robbed of their security. The permanence of a divorce—at least initially—is like the permanence of death. Divorce has made America's teens feel like orphans in their own homes.

How does God respond to a family without a father (or mother)? Hosea 14:3 says, "For in you the fatherless find compassion." He promises to be "the helper of the fatherless" (Psalm 10:14). He says He will be "a father to the fatherless, a defender of widows" (Psalm 68:5). If you have endured a divorce in your family, you have a very special place in the heart of God. He looks at you the same as He does an orphan because you have gone through many of the same things. He promises to help you and to stick with you through all the empty days and lonely nights.

If your parents are divorced and have remained single, don't take sides. You may have a tendency to favor the one you are living with because you hear his or her side of the story all the time. Just realize that it takes two to have problems. Rarely can the blame be placed on one person. Both of your parents are imperfect, so don't idolize one over the other.

If one of your parents tries to put the other down, you should politely ask that parent to stop. You shouldn't have to hear anything negative about either of your parents from anyone. And no matter what the ongoing problems may be, you should not allow yourself to be put in the middle. It is wrong for them to ask or force you to choose sides or to ask you to get in the middle of their fights. Don't fall for the "Just tell your father . . ." ploy. Remember, you're their kid, not a referee! A counselor needs to get in the middle, not you. This may take a lot of self-control because you will sometimes want to be a helper. After all, you have the blood of both parents in you. And while you should be proud of that, you shouldn't allow that fact to persuade you to take on roles that set you up for resentment.

Stepfamily Harmony

Fifteen percent of children in the United States live with stepfamilies.[1] If you are in one of those families, you know you're

◄◄ *This becomes a game to them, and you are the pawn.*

not the Lone Ranger. And you also know that not everything is going to be OK simply because there is a male and a female figure in the home. Some adults think that getting a new spouse will help to soothe the pain of the divorce. Their motive may be right, but the result does not usually accomplish what they wanted. Here are some things to watch for:

Spite-driven behavior. Many times your biological parents are still mad at each other when one or both remarry. They are so hurt, they continue to think of ways to get even with the other person for the pain he or she caused. They may tell you things about the other parent to try to get you mad at him or her. They may even try to lure you away from the other parent by buying your love and attention. This becomes a game to them, and you are the pawn. When I was a little seven-year-old, my parents divorced. Once, when I went to visit my dad, he held me up in the window of his home to kiss my stepmom while my mother was driving off!

And it's a well-used ploy for one parent to talk bad about the other's new spouse just to keep you from liking him or her. The tragedy is that all this stuff just messes with your head even more. You have to learn to see through all these games. Discern what's going on, then don't go along with their immaturity.

Guilt and a divided heart. Say you finally accept the fact that the parent you live with is remarried. (Let's say your mom in this case, just to cut down on the confusion.) You decide you are going to try to get to know your new stepdad, and you find out that he is not too bad a person after all. In fact, you even like him. While visiting your real father, you accidentally end up saying more than you should about your new relationship with your stepdad. Suddenly, you notice some jealousy on his face and in his tone of voice. Though you back-pedal quickly by playing down how much you like your stepfather, you realize you're under attack.

Inside you start feeling guilty for even liking him at all. This new relationship is what your mom has been begging for, even praying for. However, now that you really like the guy, you feel as if you are betraying your dad. It seems like whatever you do, you can't win.

Do you know that you have nothing to feel guilty about? If your biological parent is trying to make you feel bad about liking your new stepparent, it's his problem, not yours. Just because you like and perhaps want to honor your new stepparent does not mean you do not love your biological parent. All of this potential mess is a good reminder that both of your parents need to know that you love them no matter what kind of relationship you have with your stepparent.

It is easy to feel divided between your two families. You go to one house and do not feel completely at home, and you go to the other house and still do not feel like you are at home. So where is your real home, anyway? It's a lonely feeling.

Stepparent losing out. Let's go back to your mom for a moment. Remember, she finally got into a relationship after the divorce. After she remarries, you are determined not to get along with your new stepfather (we're playing "what if," remember). You make him jump through every hoop you can think of, but you've already decided that no matter what he does, he will lose. He is working hard to pay for your food, clothes, and housing. He is learning how to love not only your mom, but you and your brothers and sisters as well. He's trying to be all that you need in a father, but you don't care. You're more interested in punishing your mom for divorcing your dad than you are in allowing family harmony to return.

In the midst of a disagreement, you shout, "You're not my real dad, anyway!" A statement like that cuts to the heart of someone doing all he can to be accepted.

It's time to grow up. Life offers no promises except the one Jesus made: "In this world you will have trouble. But take heart! I have overcome the world" (John 16:33b). You have to start cutting your stepfather some slack, learn to make the best of a situation no amount of the silent treatment will change, and above all, realize that your stepfather is a person too!

Living God loud through difficult situations means asking the question, "How would Jesus treat him?" If your mom and dad are genuinely trying to do their best to pick up and go on with life, then you need to do the same by trying to see your stepparent through the eyes of God.

As a teen, I moved in with my dad and stepmother. I was fifteen and she was twenty-six. It was not my idea of a good time! We increasingly despised each other as the days turned into weeks and months. Finally, after I got turned on to the Lord, God began to draw our hearts together. I started to see her as an individual instead of a twenty-six-year-old hag who wanted to boss me around. Later she gave her heart to the Lord and asked me to baptize her. We became the best of friends, sharing what God was doing in our lives and praying together regularly. It was an incredible change!

The Making of a New Family

One day, Jesus was talking to a crowd. Someone came to Him and said, " 'Your mother and brothers are standing outside, wanting to speak to you.' He replied to him, 'Who is my mother, and who are my brothers? . . . For whoever does the will of my

◄◄ *It's time to grow up. Life offers no promises except the one Jesus made: "In this world you will have trouble. But take heart! I have overcome the world" (John 16:33b).*

Father in heaven is my brother and sister and mother'"
(Matthew 12:47–50).

You cannot go through life thinking you'll never be whole
because your family is not together anymore. Jesus had an
entirely different definition of *family* anyway. He said it was
those who really loved His Father and did His will who were His
family. It takes more than the same blood to make up a close
family. It takes a unity of heart. I know of Christian stepfamilies
that are much closer than many natural families that are still
together but do not have the Lord. It is more important to be in
God's family together than in a traditional family where your
hearts are all torn apart and you're going separate ways. Clearly,

---

◄◄ *You cannot go through life thinking you'll never be
whole because your family is not together anymore.*

Live Loud
ACTION

Jesus set a new definition and standard for the family. One that revolves around His Father. Choose to forgive Mom and Dad if they have divorced. Choose to honor them and to honor any stepparent who is in the home, because he or she has stepped in and cared for you.

Ask them to forgive any hurtful words you have shouted during an argument.

Live Loud
THOUGHT

"Be kind and compassionate to one another, forgiving each other, just as in Christ God forgave you" (Ephesians 4:32).

Live God LOUD

Chapter 12 ◎ What Would Jesus Do?
Forgiveness: Letting Go of the
Past

As you can sense from these last few chapters, in families today there are many complex issues that are causing a lot of hurt. Too many arguments and too many harsh words have been exchanged that have put a wall between young people and their parents or stepparents. It would be foolish to pretend that these situations never happened. And bad feelings will not just go away . . . unless the Lord finally becomes Lord.

To live God loud you must learn to forgive—and forget—just as the Lord has done with your own sins and offenses toward Him.

And it all must start with you.

That's right. You.

In a situation that is likely out of your control, there is only one thing you can control: your response to it all. You hold the power to get your heart right first and then hope others involved will take your lead and do the same. Life is way too

> ◀◀ *In a situation that is likely out of your control, there is only one thing you can control: your response to it all.*

short to let the wall of bitterness separate people who live under the same roof.

I've experienced firsthand the sad fact that family situations are a major source of real hurt. When the people we love most wind up hurting us through selfish or sinful choices, it stings our heart. Some of you reading these pages may have been stabbed in the back, talked about, cut down, beaten, or even sexually abused. But you are NOT without hope. This chapter will tell you how you can be whole again and how you can restore lost relationships.

Again, my firsthand experience tells me that God's awesome power can take away any pain, no matter how deep it may be. The key to your recovery lies in that powerful choice called FORGIVENESS. Instead of going through your teenage years hurting and resentful, it's important for you to make the decision to deal with your pain before you go any further. No relationship, no amount of fun, no career choice, no drug, no pleasurable activity can take away the pain of your present or your past—only forgiveness can.

When I was growing up, I had to confront head-on some forgiveness issues. What I'm about to share with you, I know from experience will work.

My Personal Battle

My mom and I had a really tough time getting along as I grew up. I felt like she was constantly out to get me. It seemed like she always punished me worse than my brothers and sisters. She would say things that made me feel so low I felt like flushing myself down the toilet. I grew up hating her. Though I somehow knew all of this hate wasn't right, I didn't have any idea how to get rid of it.

After I gave my life to the Lord, He began to deal with me

about my mom. I had to change the way I felt toward her because I had finally learned some lessons from my new faith about love and compassion. I don't remember how the message was sent, but God got through to my wounded heart and told me I had to forgive my mom. What you are about to read is exactly the process God took me through to forgive her. It worked for me, and if you have any relationship that needs restoring, this process will work for you.

When a powerless person is abused by someone more powerful, the pain is often so deep it's hard to believe that it will ever go away. Holding on to the gift of forgiveness won't affect the person who hurt you as much as it will affect you when you grasp it tightly. It's like a cancer in your heart that is slowly infecting your whole body.

The key element in dealing with hurt is wondering what can be done with all of the hurtful memories you've been back-logging. While the future *could* get better, it's the past that is hard to let go of.

Did you know that God has the power to heal your memories?

When you truly forgive, the cancer of the past not only goes into remission, it is like it has been surgically cut out of your emotions. You won't necessarily forget *every* bad thing that happened to you, but God takes away the sting and pain of those memories. It will no longer hurt to think of them.

Usually, when someone gets hurt, he or she gets mad. It is hard to distinguish between these two emotions, because both are felt at the same time. The Bible says in Ephesians 4:26–27, "'In your anger do not sin': Do not let the sun go down while you are still angry, and do not give the devil a foothold." Sure, things are going to make you mad, but you have to know how to handle your anger when it comes. Many people have grown old and bitter at the world because they let anger and bitterness overtake them. God says, do not even let *one day* go by while you are still mad. If you do, you give the devil a foothold in your life.

You can follow the Lord, go to church, and read your Bible every day. But if you get mad and stay mad, you invite the devil to put a stronghold—a fortress of pain—on part of your life. It is like you are asking him to camp out right in your living room.

Ephesians 4:31–32 tells us how to deal with anger: "Get rid of all bitterness, rage and anger, brawling and slander, along with every form of malice. Be kind and compassionate to one another, forgiving each other, just as in Christ God forgave you." You get rid of anger by forgiving. It is the only way. No matter what you have been through, God has given you the power to forgive.

How can it be done?

Memorize Scripture

You have to be ready to go to war if you really want to get rid of your pain. The way you fight this war is with God's Word. If you've dealt with abuse for months or years, the deep hurt doesn't disappear with a quick little prayer. The devil has been busy cramming guilt and condemnation down your throat for years. Now it's time to cram some TRUTH in your heart concerning forgiveness. Study scriptures like:

- ◎ "For if you forgive men when they sin against you, your heavenly Father will also forgive you" (Matthew 6:14).
- ◎ "And when you stand praying, if you hold anything against anyone, forgive him, so that your Father in heaven may forgive you your sins" (Mark 11:25).

> ◀◀ *But if you get mad and stay mad, you invite the devil to put a stronghold—a fortress of pain—on part of your life.*

- ◎ "Forgive, and you will be forgiven" (Luke 6:37).
- ◎ "I can do everything through him who gives me strength" (Philippians 4:13).

Write these and other forgiveness scriptures down on index cards and take them with you everywhere. Meditate on them until you are saying them in your sleep. This is the first step toward your wholeness.

Make a Decision to Forgive

Forgiveness is not a feeling. You will never wake up one day and think, "Boy, I feel like forgiving today!" Our natural human tendency is never to forgive.

A good definition of *forgiveness* is "giving up my right to hurt you back when you have hurt me first." The one who hurt you often deserves to have you be very angry with him. No one would argue with that. The whole idea is to give up your right to strike back.

You cannot wait for God to tell you to forgive. He has already told you that you need to forgive (see Matthew 6:14–15). Your mandate to forgive does not depend on the other person's repentant heart, either. You must forgive even if the person who hurt you never admits he did anything wrong. And it doesn't even matter if you will never see him again. A friend I know had a real jerk for his second stepfather. The man used to beat up his mom. After they divorced, my friend never saw that stepfather again. When my friend gave his life to Christ, he still had leftover hate and bitterness toward that man. Though he never got to look the man in the eye and tell him he was forgiven, he forgave him from his heart. He forgave him without seeing him.

> ◄◄ *Our natural human tendency is never to forgive.*

True forgiveness that sets your heart free is between you and God.

Once you make the decision to forgive, the heaviness begins to lift off your life. A miracle happens in your heart!

Remember Stephen, the first disciple killed for his faith? As he was being stoned, he said, "Lord, do not hold this sin against them" (Acts 7:60). Wow! Right in the middle of the stoning, he made a decision to forgive the very men who were killing him. You can decide right in the midst of people persecuting you to let go of your anger, with Jesus' power.

Fight the Battle in Your Mind

Even after you have made the decision and prayed a genuine prayer to unlock forgiveness, the battle isn't quite over. You will not necessarily feel an overwhelming love right away for the person you forgave. Forgiveness is not a feeling; it's a decision. You may think, *I don't feel any different about the person or about my pain, so I guess I didn't really forgive him.*

WRONG! If you made the decision, then you have forgiven.

Remember when you said yes to receiving the gift of forgiveness that Jesus offered? Though the fact of our choice was certain, there were likely times when you didn't *feel* forgiven. Those doubting thoughts came from the father of lies, the devil. In the same way, the devil will try to trick you into feeling condemned and confused about your decision to forgive those who hurt you. It is important to remember the date and time you forgave those people so you can remind the devil—and remind yourself—what you chose to do.

Even after you've made this important choice, you will have a natural tendency to take up the offense again and get mad. All this does is make you lose the ground you and the Lord have fought to take. Every time unforgiveness creeps back, pull out those forgiveness scripture cards and start quoting them. You see, the battle is in your mind. If you pull out God's Word every single time you are tempted to get angry again, there is NO question you will win. Though you ought to find others to encourage you, you must be prepared to fight the battle with the sword of God's Word. Use it the moment hurtful thoughts enter your brain in their vain hopes of filtering bitterness down to your will.

As you continue to wage this war—and succeed at kicking out words of death with words of LIFE—you will begin to take more ground and feel less and less pain. And believe it or not, you'll find a growing love in your heart for the person who hurt you. You will discover that the clouds are gone and you really are set free!

One last note: If you have been the victim of sexual abuse, you should confide in your pastor or a qualified Christian counselor. It is imperative that you have someone help you work through these forgiveness issues, especially before you get married. You will avoid many years of grief and marital struggles if you will take the time to do this now.

It may take weeks or months before you *feel* any different about the person who hurt you. Don't be discouraged. God's Word has the power to heal your broken heart. It NEVER fails! You just have to be committed to fighting your thoughts with His Word no matter how long it takes, because you know it's the right thing to do.

As you persist in your decision to forgive, and as you program God's Word into your memory bank, you will find the most incredible miracle happening in your heart. You will sense a freedom like you have never known before. The dark cloud of the unforgiveness cancer that surrounded you will leave. God will perform heart surgery that no world-class surgeon could ever perform. He alone has the AWESOME POWER TO HEAL A BROKEN HEART.

Your healing can begin today. It all starts with your decision to forgive.

Live Loud
ACTION

Write down ALL of the people who have ever offended or hurt you, whether they be family or friends. Now, tell the Lord about all of your anger and unforgiveness. Be honest with Him about it all in any words that come to mind. Next, ask Him to take it out of your heart. Take as long as you need.

Live Loud
THOUGHT

"If anyone says, 'I love God,' yet hates his brother, he is a liar. For anyone who does not love his brother, whom he has seen, cannot love God, whom he has not seen. And he has given us this command: Whoever loves God must also love his brother" (1 John 4:20–21).

F Section FOUR

◎ *The Hard Stuff*

There are some issues that just cannot be categorized other than by calling them HARD STUFF. Today's teens are dealing with things that just a decade ago nobody even knew existed. And most of these hard situations have an effect on their desire and ability to live God loud.

If teenagers are going to rise above the things that would try to bog them down, they are going to have to face these issues head-on. I'm convinced that all teenagers—no matter what they're going through—can start to let Jesus Christ and their Christian faith affect every area of their lives. No more tiptoeing around or avoiding tough issues.

In the following chapters are a number of bold-faced decisions that teenagers—perhaps even you—have to make in order to live God loud.

⏮ *If teenagers are going to rise above the things that would try to bog them down, they are going to have to face these issues head-on.*

Live God LOUD

Chapter 13 ◎ Why Do I Feel So Rotten?
Teenage Bubonic Plague:
Inferiority

Arising from an overpopulation of disease-ridden rats, the bubonic plague caused death to millions of people throughout Europe in the Middle Ages. It was known as the Black Death because as death approached, people's skin would turn gray.

There is an epidemic running rampant throughout this country. It has the potential to infect the heart and home of every junior-high and high-school student in this nation. From major cities to grass-roots American towns, this disease of the heart is taking a horrific toll.

This plague, however, doesn't kill your body . . . it kills your dreams. It stifles your potential. It makes you feel like a loser before you've even had a chance to enter the game. Many teens feel unloved and unwanted as a result of this peril.

It's called *inferiority*.

Peak years for major depression are between ages fifteen and nineteen. Rates of depression during those years are two to four times higher than in middle age and up to seven times higher than after age sixty-five.[1] As a result of feeling so low, millions of young teenagers try alcohol, drugs, or other pursuits to help numb the hurt. Some will do anything to temporarily take away the sting, if only for a little while, of feeling like a nothing. While our world will continue its search to look for ways to control the drug and alcohol problem, I believe this won't ever be accomplished until we solve the esteem problem.

God's Goal for You!

God wants to do great things through you in your teen years, not to mention your whole life. It is mind-boggling to imagine the awesome things He has prepared for you. The problem is that too many teenagers end up never pursuing the things God has for them simply because they *don't think they can*.

Why do they think like this?

For decades, the media has held up idols and heroes whom, we're led to believe, we should emulate. As the parade of stars from the world of TV, movies, sports, and music walks by before us, it's nearly impossible NOT to compare ourselves with them.

As guys we are taught to look up to athletic role models on the court and field, and to the macho movie heroes on the silver screen. We believe the definition of a real man is found next to the word *muscle* in the dictionary. Given the choice of having Bill Gates's money or Matt Damon's looks (and the girls who come with it), looks and brawn would almost always win out.

We guys somehow believe that if we do not have hair on our chest and cannot bench-press 250 pounds by the time we are fifteen years old, we are not really men. No guy says it, but millions are thinking it: *Something must be wrong with ME.* Add this to the immoral beliefs given to you by the pop culture, mixed with peer pressure, and suddenly you think you're strange if

◄◄ *It makes you feel like a loser before you've even had a chance to enter the game.*

you aren't sleeping with someone early in your teen years. The result: You've got A LOT of mixed-up teenage guys.

In my mind, Jesus was the only real man who ever lived. That's why I'm constantly looking at the example He set. His passion was to be like His heavenly Father in every way. He knew it wasn't outer strength that made the man, but the inner strength of imitating the Almighty God! Can He also be the ultimate example for a girl? Absolutely!

Hollywood and Madison Avenue (the marketing capital of the world) say a girl must have looks and curves to be worth anything. Nearly every magazine that targets teenage females leaves a girl feeling like she must look like those models or she just can't possibly survive her teen years. Have you ever wondered how all of those models look so perfect? The model they put on the front cover of a magazine has gone through four- to six-hour makeup sessions. A small army of stylists has worked over her hair, and her wardrobe has been extensively prepared. Then she spent hours and hours at a photo shoot and had literally thousands of pictures taken, only to have one chosen for the cover. Even after the absolutely best photo is selected, the image is put on a sophisticated computer and enhanced even further, eliminating all of the model's flaws.

The picture then appears on the front of the magazine, where you see it and say in your heart, "I wish I looked like that!" The *model* wishes she looked like that!

It is a fake representation of reality. No one looks that good without a lot of work! Even your brother could look like that if he had that many people working on him. Meanwhile, most teenage girls are left feeling like they do not measure up, like they will *never* measure up.

Have you ever heard a girl say, "I'm fat!"? You are looking at her thinking, *Girl, you are so skinny, you're going to blow away if I sneeze!* Maybe you have heard a beautiful girl say, "I am so ugly!"

Before she finishes, most guys are thinking, *Baby, baby, baby, haven't you ever looked in the mirror?* These types of statements prove the obvious: It does not matter what people look like on the outside; if they feel worthless inside, they'll think they don't measure up.

More evidence of this plague is made known when people ask, "How do I look?" or "Do you think I'm pretty?" all the time. Of course everyone likes to get a compliment, but some people are constantly fishing for them. They think that if they can get enough people to say they are OK, then they will actually feel OK. But it's not true. No matter how many compliments you get, the problem is not cured.

Sometimes it is our friends or family who make us feel like a nothing. The people you love can hurt you the worst by the words they say because you value their opinion so much. Just one comment like "Boy, are you dumb!" from your dad is enough to make you feel like you need to go to a learning disability class.

Finally, there is the church. Tragically, many people are taught that God thinks they are worms. They are led to believe that it is a good practice of humility to think they are nothing but insignificant specks of dust to God and that they should grovel in the dirt and beg for mercy. After all, doesn't the Bible say, "Humble yourselves before the Lord, and he will stomp your head" (James 4:10)?

Read again.

It says, " . . . he will lift you up"! That is the kind of God He is! He lifts you up because He thinks you are more valuable than any other creations.

> ◀◀ *It does not matter what people look like on the outside; if they feel worthless inside, they'll think they don't measure up.*

So, if you get all these messages from the media, your family, and your friends telling you that you are not worth much, and then you hear it from a preacher, it just looks as if the evidence is conclusive. You think, *Well, if God thinks I'm a loser, too, then I must really be one!*

Have you ever seen a perfect-looking car belching smoke? It may look incredible on the outside, but the engine—the thing that actually makes the car run—is about to fall off its mounts. Unless it's a show car that never has its tires touch a real highway, it's useless. And unless you just want a "show life," never being truly useful in the hands of the Master, you've got to get past the external image and the lies people say and start hearing and believing the truth.

Is it time for you to fix up the inside so you can genuinely feel good about the person God made?

What Did Jesus Say about It?

Matthew 22:37–39 says, "Jesus replied: 'Love the Lord your God with all your heart and with all your soul and with all your mind.' This is the first and greatest commandment. And the second is like it: 'Love your neighbor as yourself.'"

Jesus is clear about what our priorities should be. He says the first thing is that we should love God with all we've got. The second command is just like it. In other words, it is so important that Jesus could not say the first one without mentioning the second one. He said you should "love your neighbor as *yourself.*"

Many people think this means you should love everyone else but not love yourself. They make a priority list that looks like this:

1. Love God.
2. Love others.
3. Love yourself.

If you look closer, that's not really what Jesus said. He said to love others *as* you love yourself. That means that you must love others equally—as much as you love yourself. Did you know that if you cannot love yourself, you cannot love others? Oh, you can try, but it never really comes across as love.

It sounds strange to say that we should "love ourselves." In fact, it sounds kind of prideful to say, "I love myself." Some might say, "Isn't that conceit and pride?" No, it is not. When we say, "Boy, that guy sure loves himself a lot," what we really mean is, "He is arrogant." Arrogance comes from low self-esteem. He, the arrogant one, feels so low about himself that he tries to make others believe that he is really something marvelous. He tries to push others around and make them feel weaker with his comments. He is the kind of person who really *does not* love himself. If he did, he would not feel he had to prove himself to anyone.

You can only love others as much as you love yourself. Anything else is just a vain servant or martyr mentality that makes you feel good the more you put yourself down. Look at what Jesus told Peter in Luke 5:8. Peter said to Jesus, "Go away from me, Lord; I am a sinful man!" He had the same mentality that many people have today. "Go away from me, Lord; I'm ugly, dirty, and worthless." That's how a lot of us felt when we first discovered that Jesus was real. We have a tendency to push God away when we realize He is holy and we are not. But look at Jesus' response: "Don't be afraid; from now on you will catch men" (Luke 5:10). He was saying to Peter, "I don't want you to push yourself away from Me. Come toward Me. Do not be afraid. And I will give you a mission in life that is perfectly suited for you!"

It was nearly a rebuke. "Peter! Get up off the ground! Stop that groveling! Quit crying and saying how worthless you are." Jesus said, "From now on you will be fishing for men!" He was telling Peter, "I see a great future for you. Now, stand up like a man! See yourself the way I see you. You are not a worm; you are going to do great things for God!"

Jesus asked the woman caught in adultery, "Woman, where are they [her accusers]? Has no one condemned you? . . . Then neither do I condemn you. . . . Go now and leave your life of sin" (John 8:10–11). He took a woman who had a lot of reasons to feel ashamed and worthless and restored her dignity. If Jesus went out of His way to make her feel valuable, what does He think of you?

He thinks you can be the greatest!

It is not a sin to love yourself. It is holy. It is right. Jesus said it is the most important thing after loving God! It is more of a sin NOT to love yourself, because you are denying the truth of who God made you to be.

If you're convinced it's OK to love yourself, here's how to get started.

Stopping the Epidemic

There is only one cure. You have to believe the truth about yourself. God created you in His image. He does not make junk! The Bible says that He "knit [you] together in [your] mother's womb and . . . [you] are fearfully and wonderfully made" (Psalm 139:13–14)! He got really excited the day you were born, because you were another awesome example of His creation.

Now you have a choice to make. You can believe Hollywood or you can believe God. You can believe *Vogue* or *Cosmopolitan* magazine or you can believe the Bible. The world wants to run your self-esteem into the ground; God wants to lift you up. If you think about it, if you believe what the world says, by your thoughts and actions you are calling God a liar. You are saying, "I don't care what You say, Lord; I still believe that I'm a loser."

So what do you do now? You start with repenting. That's right, repenting. "But," you say, "I'm already a Christian." That's great, but you still need to turn away from your old way of thinking. You need to change your mind, to turn around. You need to ask God to forgive you for calling Him a liar. You need to commit to believing the truth and speaking the truth about yourself.

You need to say to yourself, "Self, I don't care how you feel; I don't care what the world says. If God says I am valuable, then I am going to believe what He says about me instead of what I have always thought."

I love to tease people who wear mink coats. I always make a joke about the coat being dog hair. I will say something like, "What a beautiful dog-hair coat you have. What was his name, anyway?" I'm basically joking about something that is really valuable and calling it worthless. Sometimes we're tempted to do the same thing to the Lord, only it is not quite as funny. We call ourselves worthless, when in fact we have been washed in the mink coat of Jesus' blood.

An object is worth whatever you are willing to pay for it. When I go overseas to different countries, I love to bargain for things. Now, if I leave the market after paying five dollars for a souvenir, to me that thing is worth five bucks. If I lost the souvenir, I would think I had lost five dollars' worth of stuff. When God decided to buy you back from the bondage of your sin, He thought about what to pay for you. He could have paid with all the diamonds and oil in the earth. But those were not enough. He could have traded land or a country full of cash. But even this was not enough. When He decided your value, His love knew of only one choice. He brought His own Son on the scene to shed His blood. That's how much you're worth to God, the blood of His only Son!

My Life

As I said earlier, I grew up feeling pretty low. I felt like a complete failure, like I would never make anything out of my life. Even after I gave my heart to the Lord when I was sixteen, I still felt like a loser. I was the guy everyone picked on in school. Finally, I got hold of one scripture that changed my life. I had read it a million times before, but finally it came alive to me: "I can do everything through him who gives me strength" (Philippians 4:13). And though in context the verse is talking about living rich or living poor, this truth has a thousand applications. I read it again and again! I couldn't believe God was telling ME that He believed in me! ME!! Ron Luce could do all things through Christ! I thought, *Lord, in the midst of a world that has always told me I can't do anything with my life, here You are telling me I can do all things!*

From that point, I had a choice to make. I could believe what I always thought was true, or I could believe what God said was true. I thought, *God, if You said it about me, then I don't care what anyone else says; I'm going to believe what You say.* My life was completely changed that day. I looked up every scripture I could find about who God said I was, and I began to repeat them back to myself. I thought, *If God can say it about me, then I can say it about me too!*

God wants to use you to change your world. Don't you dare let the inferiority the world tries to cram down your throat shut you down! Choose today to believe what God says about you! You will never be the same!

Live Loud
ACTION

Memorize the "Live Loud Thought" below.

Live Loud
THOUGHT

"For you created my inmost being; you knit me together in my mother's womb. I praise you because I am fearfully and wonderfully made; your works are wonderful, I know that full well. . . . How precious to me are your thoughts, O God! How vast is the sum of them! Were I to count them, they would outnumber the grains of sand. When I awake, I am still with you" (Psalm 139:13–14, 17–18).

Live God LOUD

Chapter 14 ◉ Why Does God Care about What I Listen To? The People behind the Tunes

To live God loud, your relationship with Jesus should affect every area of your life. If He really came to live through you, then His ways, His thoughts, and His ideas should begin affecting every area of your life . . . including an area as sensitive as music.

Who Invented Music?

What is music? Why was it invented?

Well, if you look back to Judges 5:3, it says, "I will sing to the LORD, I will sing; I will make music to the LORD, the God of Israel." As you read through the Bible, you see it talks about angels making music to the Lord in heaven, complete with trumpets blasting and harps playing. Music was invented to glorify God. It was invented as a way of expressing His majesty. Today we have music played by every culture and religion.

Let me clarify a couple of things: First of all, there is nothing wrong with music. It was created to glorify God. The problem comes in the people who are expressing themselves in the music. Because what most musicians express does not honor God.

Some Christians believe that certain styles of music, such as rock-'n'-roll or heavy metal, are wrong. But style is not the issue. It is the *content* and the *spirit* behind the music that is the issue.

Secular musicians write songs based on their particular perspectives, the particular experiences they have had—good or bad times, experiences with drugs or alcohol, or acts of immorality. Sometimes they are trying to prove a point; other times they are just expressing a thought or an idea that they have in their head.

These musicians have taken the gifts that God gave them and are using them for themselves. Actually, they are often using them for the devil, because many times they are presenting ideas that are not from the Lord. And if they are not from the Lord, then there is only one other source.

The problem for teens in this whole issue is the control factor. Most teens have control over their own music choices, and they don't want anyone telling them what to do.

Here's my dilemma with secular music: If these musicians don't know the Lord and are still slaves to sin, or are rebellious against God or don't want to have anything to do with Him, then they are writing music out of the old nature. And no matter what someone says, when you listen to music, you are letting it influence your mind. It is going in your ears, then into your head, and it won't be long before you begin to think about the words.

Remember what Paul said in Romans 12:2: "Do not conform any longer to the pattern of this world, but be transformed by the renewing of your mind. Then you will be able to test and approve what God's will is—his good, pleasing and perfect will." If you have your mind renewed by the Scriptures and then

⏮ *Style is not the issue. It is the CONTENT and the SPIRIT behind the music that is the issue.*

go back to listening to secular music, you are simply tearing down the Word of God that has been planted.

The Power of the Subculture

American and European styles of music have their own subculture. When I was a teenager in the late '70s, heavy metal was just beginning. By the early '80s it was firmly entrenched throughout America. How could you tell? Most of the listeners tried to dress like their favorite metal group. The same is true today of those who listen to Goth or death metal music. Its followers dress and even dance like the performers do in concerts and in music videos.

When a group within a culture acts and speaks in a distinct way, that group becomes a subculture. It is a small group within a group. Those who constantly listen to Goth music may not even realize that they wear black all the time, do their hair a certain way, have a certain attitude, or say certain words their music uses. The subculture has sucked them in, and they don't even realize it. Slowly, they are unconsciously being trained to think the way their subculture thinks, to sing the way it sings, to look the way it looks, and to act the way it acts.

The Bible speaks very clearly about this in Exodus 23:2. It says, "Do not follow the crowd in doing wrong." Do not give in to peer pressure. Do not do what the world wants you to do just because the world wants you to do it.

I could give dozens of examples of present-day music groups who are using their creative talents to preach a gospel of self, a gospel of immorality, a gospel of lies. If I did, however, this book would be outdated within a year because new groups are coming up so often, you can't keep track of who is really current. But you're probably discerning enough to know when a group has good lyrics or raunchy ones, if you'll take the time to look.

If you listen to secular music, what ends up happening (whether you admit it or not) is that you let those groups influence what you think, what is cool and not cool, and what you do with the temple of the Holy Spirit (your body). They are ripping you off, and most listeners do not even realize it. You have to be strong and realize that their philosophies are working their way into the way you think and the way you live.

You need to begin to measure the music you listen to by its words and to compare them to the Word of God. If the music agrees with the Word, then listen to it. If not, do not listen to it because you'll eventually be tricked into believing it. It doesn't happen on the first listen; it happens slowly (the devil is patient) as you listen to the music over and over again. The result: Your foundation in Christ will become unstable.

Now is the time for you to get honest about getting rid of some of the music you listen to. If you have been wondering why you have been going up and down in your Christian walk, your music could be the reason. Do you have the strength to do what is right?

I want you to strongly consider losing ALL of your secular music. You read right. All.

As you can tell, this is not a casual suggestion. I firmly believe that for most teens it is a matter of spiritual survival. And I'm just as convinced that God will honor your courageous stand and bless you if you give your music life to Him.

MTV Influence

MTV has given free access to hundreds of bands that promote a lifestyle that mocks everything the Bible stands for.

MTV is in more than 400 million households worldwide (CNN is only in 150 million).[1] The producers proudly proclaim that it is a "cultural force. People don't watch it—they live it.

MTV has affected the way a whole generation thinks, talks, and buys."

Yet they boast that they "listen to this generation and give them what they want." It looks more like they are manipulating a generation for their own gains.

Again, they boast, "The strongest appeal you can make is emotional. If you can make them forget their logic, you've got 'em. At MTV we don't shoot for the fourteen-year-olds, we own them."

So, how do you like someone telling you he owns you?

The problem is that on any given week 42 percent of Christian teens watch MTV compared to only 30 percent of non-Christian teens.[2]

What Are We Gonna Do about It?

When I talk about music, do I mean that instead of listening to music with secular lyrics you should listen only to church songs or hymns?

No, that's not what I'm saying.

I'm saying that music is an expression of your heart, an expression of an idea, an expression of something that you are thinking about or something that is going on inside of you. People write songs about the things that inspire them.

The Bible says that if you are going to sing a song, let it be a spiritual song: "Sing and make music in your heart to the Lord" (Ephesians 5:19).

Let the song talk about:

◎ how awesome God is

◎ how cool God is

◎ how great God is

Don't waste your energy glorifying someone else's ideas, an experience somebody else had, or another way of looking at life. Sing songs that lift up the King of kings and Lord of lords.

As we have already said, there is nothing wrong with the style of music itself. The important thing is: Who wrote the stuff you are pumping into your head? What was in his heart when he wrote it? Because this is what's going to get in your heart when you listen to it.

God has raised up many different music styles with people who have given their lives to Jesus. Try pumping this stuff into your brains instead, and see what happens!

Any Limits?

I sincerely believe that it is really important not to just blow your brains out with loud, wild (even Christian) stuff ALL THE TIME. No matter who you are or what style of music you like, it is imperative that you slow down and listen to some worship songs as well. Take the busyness and loudness out of your life long enough to give God quality attention from your heart. Who knows, you might actually hear HIS voice if you quiet everything else down! The point is, to live God loud, you can't be distracted with constant noise. You have to get quiet once in a while and let God's still, small voice speak to your heart. There is no comparison between having God speak to you and the constant clutter from music and MTV.

> ◄◄ *No matter who you are or what style of music you like, it is imperative that you slow down and listen to some worship songs as well. Take the busyness and loudness out of your life long enough to give God quality attention from your heart.*

Live Loud
ACTION

Send a letter (like the one below) to MTV and let them know what you think they are doing to this world's teenagers: MTV, Attn: Viewer Services, 1515 Broadway, New York, NY 10036.

> Date:
>
> Dear MTV:
>
> My name is _____. I want to let you know that you DO NOT own me! I will NOT watch your network. I am tired of all the sick videos (sex, violence, and drug abuse), as well as the other programming that portrays rebellion and lifestyles that have proven to wreck people's lives.
>
> I am unplugging you from my home, and I am calling my cable company to ask that you be disconnected from our cable system.
>
> When you begin to use your influence to shape my generation with some wholesome values, I will be happy to plug you back in.
>
> Sincerely, _____
>
> age _____

Live Loud
THOUGHT

"For from within, out of men's hearts, come evil thoughts, sexual immorality, theft, murder, adultery, greed, malice, deceit, lewdness, envy, slander, arrogance and folly. All these evils come from inside and make a man 'unclean' " (Mark 7:21–23).

Live God LOUD

Chapter 15 ◎ Why Can't I Live My Own Life?
Peer Pressure: Feeling Good about Not Fitting In

One of the strongest forces on teenagers today is the pressure they feel from others their own age, usually from friends at school. This pressure can manipulate, change, and even completely rearrange a person's lifestyle. The power of this pressure causes teens to fix their hair differently, wear different clothes, and change the way they spend their free time. It even begins to dictate the things young people do when their parents are not around . . . things that could drastically damage their future!

Countless teens have begun smoking, drinking, shooting up, snorting, or somehow getting drugs into their system, just because of the pressure they have felt from others their age. Too many have lost their dreams, their hopes, their goals, and even their lives by doing something that so-called "friends" put pressure on them to do.

Maybe you remember the story from a TV newsmagazine about Robert. He wanted to join a gang. He was eleven years old and grew up in the Chicago area. His so-called "friends" in the gang said that he needed to kill someone if he wanted to join. So Robert took a gun and killed a fourteen-year-old girl.

The police discovered that Robert had killed the girl and that the gang "friends" had put him up to it. The gang members got scared, so they took Robert out and shot him in the head. His life was destroyed because of his so-called "friends."

Why?

One of the biggest reasons why young people give in to pressure—whether they like to admit it or not—is their desire for acceptance from others their age. Everyone wants to be liked by others. The struggle is: What will you do to get them to like you? How low will you stoop to please them? If you have to stoop so low that you go against what you believe, tell me, is getting their approval worth more than how low you feel when you compromise your standards? Hear the words of a friend of mine named Catherine:

> My insecurity started at the ripe age of eight. I was not the perfect weight like all the other "normal girls." I started believing I had to totally conform to the image of my peers and could never be accepted until I was completely like them. I always knew that I wasn't being me, but that was not a bother just as long as I had friends. I continued this belief all the way through junior high and high school. By this time I was totally immersed in all of the peer pressure games. If someone asked me to do something outrageous I'd do it because I wanted to be popular. A short time later I became consumed by drugs, alcohol, and guys. Christ was not even a hobby. Sure I went to church, but Christ

◄◄ *The core problem of peer pressure is that teens are getting their self-worth from their peers rather than from God.*

never captured my heart, soul, mind, and strength. Every day I lived in insecurity fearing that if I didn't give in to my friends' expectations, the popular me would no longer exist. My weight issue consumed me. I was always on a diet, and constantly worried about what everyone thought of my looks. I lived in fear of hearing the word "Pig!" be referenced to me.

Since I have been awake in Christ for some time now, I know how far God has brought me out. Every day He shows me how truly beautiful I am in Him. He's taught me that it doesn't matter what "Jill" or "Brianna" thinks. It only matters that He thinks I am "fearfully and wonderfully made."

Now when I have peer pressure to do something wrong I go right after God's advice. His Word on who I am is better than any suggestion an advice column in a beauty magazine can give. It tells me that I was made beautiful and perfect in God's image and that my true security comes from Christ.

Insecurity causes teens to do things they normally wouldn't do. They want so badly for others to like them that they forget all about things they value. Equating self-worth with the number of people who like them, they believe that if the popular people at school don't accept them, they must not be worth much.

The core problem of peer pressure is that teens are getting their self-worth from their peers rather than from God.

As we discussed in chapter 13, if you know what God thinks of you, it won't matter what others say about you. You have to believe God's opinion more than you believe the opinions of other teens around you. You have to choose to value His thoughts about you more than you value their thoughts.

How to Stand Up against Peer Pressure

Here are some ideas on how you can stand up against peer pressure:

Know you are right. The story of Shadrach, Meshach, and Abednego gives you a perfect plan of action to follow when you are faced with peer pressure. If you remember, in Daniel 3, King Nebuchadnezzar made a huge statue of himself and commanded everyone to bow down and worship it whenever they heard certain music. Talk about peer pressure! The whole country had to do the same thing, not just a few friends from school!

Just imagine Shadrach and his buddies thinking about this new law. As Jews, they were supposed to worship only one God, never some idol made out of a precious metal. What's more, they had each made a commitment to God to serve and honor Him alone. They knew that not obeying the king's command was the right thing to do, even if EVERY SINGLE PERSON in the country worshiped the idol.

Have you ever wondered if what you are doing is right, especially when you see almost everyone else doing the opposite? Tiffany did. Her school district declared itself a "no-prayer" zone. That meant that students were not allowed to bow their heads or close their eyes to pray, whether it was out loud or silently. After the edict was handed down, none of Tiffany's Christian friends would bow their heads to say a prayer before the lunch meal. Though Tiffany was a cheerleader and knew that disobeying the edict might cost her a spot on the squad, she wanted to honor God more than she wanted to be popular. Without fanfare, she bowed her head and prayed for fifteen silent seconds before her meal. The first day, no one noticed. The second day, however, a lunchroom monitor spotted her and told the school administration. Tiffany was immediately suspended for three days and was told that when she returned she wasn't to pray at school again.

Well, she took her punishment, but when she came back to school, her head was bowed and eyes were closed as usual.

This is where the story gets exciting. Not only was Tiffany suspended again—this time for two weeks—but she was kicked off the cheerleading squad! Her friends took notice of her stand, and the day after her second suspension, they had a prayer-in at lunch. Nearly every student bowed to say a prayer before their meal! The monitor couldn't record all of the names. Finally, a few parents got involved and took the matter to the school board. Voluntary silent prayer was restored, and Tiffany was put back on the cheerleading squad. It's amazing what God can do to help a teen reverse the pressure from the world.

You have to have confidence that living for God is the right thing to do. You do not want to be arrogant, just confident. Living God loud, passionately going after Jesus, is the BEST thing you can do with your life. Living totally pure and holy before God is the only thing that matters. Just because there are a lot more who don't care about purity does not mean they are correct. So do not be intimidated by a crowd who has been deceived and is following the wrong voice.

Make a decision beforehand. Shadrach and his friends knew they were going to be asked to bow before the idol. They did not pretend that the king would never play the music. They were realistic about it. They knew they were going to have to make a choice.

Sometimes Christian teens believe they won't face the temptations that everyone else faces. They do not realize that they are walking right into a temptation extravaganza every time they go to school.

Shadrach made his decision beforehand. He knew exactly that he and his friends would not bow to an idol. They did not wait until the heat of the moment and just make something up when the time came; they had a plan.

This is a great idea for you. Plan out in advance how to respond to your peers. Think about what you will say when someone invites you to a party where you know alcohol will be present. Know exactly what to say when someone teases you about not being sexually involved before you are married. Rehearse in your mind everyone laughing at you because of your "live God loud" stand for Him, and know what you will say (or not say) in response to them.

If you pray and talk to your other Christian friends, God will give you some one-liners that will pierce the heart of your accusers. Jesus had some of the greatest one-liners in the world! In fact, I have found that it becomes a lot more fun to be different and not fit in, just to see how your one-liners will affect the people trying to tell you how to live.

Be willing to do whatever it takes. Like everyone else, Shadrach, Meshach, and Abednego knew what the penalty was for not worshiping the king's statue. The king had announced that "whoever does not fall down and worship will immediately be thrown into a blazing furnace" (Daniel 3:6). There would be no second chance for Shadrach and his friends, but they stood firm anyway. The king brought them in and gave them a chance to follow his order, but they responded by saying one of the most courageous, convincing lines ever said by young people (remember, they were young like you).

"If we are thrown into the blazing furnace, the God we serve is able to save us from it, and he will rescue us from your hand, O king. But even if he does not, we want you to know, O king, that we will not serve your gods or worship the image of gold you have set up" (Daniel 3:17–18).

They were willing to die for what was right. Are you? Even if it costs you everything, will you go for it? It is only when you make the decision to go for it no matter what it costs you that you really experience the freedom of living for Jesus. Your willingness to follow Him—no matter what—is exactly what He asked for when you gave Him your life.

You have to realize you are in a war. So get ready to fight! Most of the people in this world are on the losing side, and they do not even know it. When you are in a war, you have to do whatever it takes to win. You have to have the determination that no matter what your peers do, you will not back down. After all, what is the worst thing they could do to you? Kill you? I think not. What are they going to do, call you a name? Oh, no! Those big mean people! Do you think they will spit on you? So what?

If you know that God approves of you, it does not really matter if anyone else approves of you or not!

Surround yourself with "live God loud" friends. If you noticed, Shadrach was not alone in his decision to stand up for what he believed. He had his friends—Meshach and Abednego—on his right and on his left. They were a threesome. They had made a commitment to God, and they stood together.

You cannot try to live the Christian life by yourself. You cannot be successful if your best friends are not saved or if they are halfhearted Christians. If the only time you see other Christian teenagers is at youth group, then you have the wrong group of friends at school. If you are stuck right in the middle of intense peer pressure at school every single day, all by yourself, it is going to be easy to fall for the temptation to follow the crowd.

If Shadrach had been hanging out with a group of people who were bowing down to the statue, it would have been harder for him to stand for what was right. If Meshach and Abednego had bowed to the idol, Shadrach might also have fallen to his knees.

> ◄◄ *You cannot try to live the Christian life by yourself. You cannot be successful if your best friends are not saved or if they are halfhearted Christians.*

The same is true for you. If you are hanging around those who are involved in stupid, sinful stuff all the time, you will get sucked into it too.

Create righteous peer pressure. Because Shadrach and his pals kept their commitment, God blew away their enemies. You probably remember that when they got thrown into the furnace they did not even get singed. In fact, they had a visitor.

The king looked in and said, "Look! I see four men walking around in the fire, unbound and unharmed, and the fourth looks like a son of the gods" (Daniel 3:25). The Bible doesn't say it specifically, but I believe Jesus had come to hang out with them in the fire. He will come and hang out with you every time you are persecuted too!

The king said, "Come out!" Nebuchadnezzar wanted to know what kind of men these guys were. What was it about them that made them not bow when everyone else did? And why weren't they burned to a crisp when they were thrown in the fire? And just who was this fourth guy, anyway? After spending some time talking with these three amazing young guys, he made a law that everyone must worship the God of Shadrach, Meshach, and Abednego! He demanded that no one say anything against their God! Then he promoted them to his staff! How is that for righteous peer pressure?

We, as Christians, need to start exerting godly, righteous peer pressure. As we stand up for God, He will vindicate us in front of our friends. In other words, He will start proving that He is right and that we are right for following Him. When your friends start seeing God's blessing on your life—how you have peace and confidence no matter what—they will want what you have. When they see that you stand for what you believe no matter what it costs you, they will know that you have something that is real.

After all, this is not just a matter of "What I believe is better than what you believe." You believe the truth—the only way to heaven. You don't just believe words written thousands of years ago; you have a relationship with a living God. Since you have given your life to Jesus, He is living inside you right now. He has changed you from the inside out!

It is time for every young person who calls himself a Christian to stand up like Shadrach, Meshach, and Abednego and be counted. Show this world that you are more serious about your walk with God than the rest of the world is about the things they believe.

It feels great to be on the right team. All the angels, the awesome forefathers (like Abraham and others), and the Father, Son, and Holy Spirit are on your side. If you have their approval, who else's approval do you really need, anyway?

Live Loud ACTION

Pick out two situations that you are tempted to fail in at school, situations that force you to compromise your faith. Go back and read Daniel 3. Then look again at points one through five on the previous pages. Decide now how you will respond to the situations that trip you up.

Live Loud THOUGHT

"What, then, shall we say in response to this? If God is for us, who can be against us? He who did not spare his own Son, but gave him up for us all—how will he not also, along with him, graciously give us all things?" (Romans 8:31–32).

Live God LOUD

Chapter 16 ◎ What Captures My Time and Attention Most? Idol Infatuation 2000

id you know that hundreds, perhaps thousands, of people are in competition for your time? For some hours of the day there is an all-out bidding war . . . for thirty ticks of the second hand! Companies are spending millions of advertising dollars . . . on you. They know that if they can capture your attention, you might spend a lot more time, and eventually your money, on whatever they're trying to sell. It's all about marketing: making products look bigger than life in order to take your money.

And what happens when you finally get that product in your house? The car, the video game, the stereo, the clothes . . . they all have the ability to capture your attention. Though it may be for only a short time, it's easy to get temporarily mesmerized. And when one possession after another captures your time, what has happened? You have, in essence, worshiped idols (one after another).

Anything like this that takes your focus away from God is an idol. The dictionary defines *idol* as: "An image of a god used as an instrument of worship, any object of excessive devotion or admiration." That may not describe those new high-top Nike basketball shoes, but it just might. Some teens spend more time taking care of their shoes than they do reading their Bibles. Tell me, is that excessive devotion?

Though worship is usually defined in terms of church or singing, there are a lot of ways to revere, to extremely devote, or to intensely love something you buy. Do you catch the problem? The only thing that deserves this kind of love and devotion is God.

Baal in Scripture

Baal was a god worshiped by the Canaanites in the Old Testament. They believed he would bring them the right weather for good crops. The Jews were commanded by God to get rid of all the gods like this when they moved in and took over the land, but they failed to do so.

The Canaanite people worshiped the idol of Baal in a number of different ways. They made sacrifices to statues of him, gave money to him as a sacrifice, and sometimes offered human sacrifices to him. The priests of Baal danced with frantic shouts and cut themselves with knives to excite the attentions and compassion of the god. Their entire lives revolved around this man-made idol.

You'd think that the Jews, God's chosen people, would be immune to following after other gods, but there they were, joining in with people who had no knowledge of the living God . . . worshiping a carved statue. These statues of Baal were scattered all throughout Israel so that virtually all Jews who wanted to worship this false god had plenty of opportunities to do so. At any

---

◄◄ *And when one possession after another captures your time, what has happened? You have, in essence, worshiped idols (one after another).*

time they could get sucked into spending their time and letting their life revolve around something that was a lie.

Today's Baals

Today we have lots of inanimate objects that steal our time and devotion.

Idols like:

Discmans. Many teens constantly keep their earphones plugged into a portable CD player or cassette deck. Their time revolves around which CD they're going to listen to next.

TV/VCR. More hours are spent in front of a TV than are spent in a classroom! Many Americans schedule their lives around what is on the tube. They faithfully watch a particular show as if the program counted on them. Many take pride in the fact that "I always watch my program!" They would never let anything interrupt their viewing schedule!

Video games. If a guy doesn't have a high-tech Sega or Nintendo in the home, then there's a Game Boy for the car. Millions of teens spend hour upon hour in a frenzied competitive daze in front of a screen.

Computers. Teens and adults alike are being pulled onto the fast lane of the information superhighway. So much is becoming available for computers that you have to make it your religion to keep up with the technology.

Cars. Getting a car becomes the goal and central pivotal point of teenagers' entire existence. They see their life as "pre-car" or "post-car." Unless Mom and Dad foot the bill, all their savings, time, and attention are put toward that first set of wheels. Then, once they get it, they pour all their money into maintaining it.

Money. Poor people and rich alike are controlled by money. The poor are controlled by money because they think about it so much—they wish they had it and dream about what they would do with it. The rich are consumed by worry that they might lose it or that someone is going to rip them off.

Non-"Possession" Idols

Idols don't have to be something you can hold in your hand; they can be people you look up to:

Music stars. Musicians are idolized like gods. While in concert surrounded by lights, sound, and video screens, they're bigger than life. And to take the experience home with them, people buy CDs, videos, shirts, buttons, and posters.

Even Christian music stars are idolized. Yes, the Christian artists may have good hearts and good ministries, and they may play good music, but this is no reason to worship them. They are human beings, saved by grace and simply trying to minister. When we put these artists on such high pedestals, we put extreme pressure on them to somehow live up to the world's ideas of a music idol.

Movie stars. We see celebrities on the silver screen and somehow they look invincible. Who wouldn't look up to someone who always got the girl (or the guy) or who can kill fifty people without getting a scratch?

Sports personalities. Many athletes seem bigger than life. Their incredible talents make them legendary. Their faces grace the cover of magazines and cereal boxes, and you see them repeatedly in clips on *SportsCenter*. Countless hours every week are devoted to watching sports on TV, and people think, "After all, anybody who makes that much money must be pretty extraordinary, right?"

Boyfriends and girlfriends. Many young people have made an idol of the one with whom they are romantically involved (or the one with whom they wish they had a romantic involvement). They "worship the ground" he or she walks on. They will do whatever they have to do to please the person, even if it violates their own principles.

What am I trying to say?

I'm not condemning everything, believe me. All of us are going to like famous people, and we're going to give our attention to what we're interested in. But there are a few questions we should ask about everything that gets our attention:

◎ Are we using them, or are they using us?
◎ Are we taking advantage of them, or are they taking advantage of us?
◎ Do we own them, or do they own us?

Basically, we are asking, Have we let that person (or thing) become the central figure around which our whole life revolves?

If so, it is probably an idol.

To live God loud, our lives can only revolve around one person, Jesus Christ. He wants to be the only thing in the center of our heart!

Do you revere, honor, and show extreme devotion to anything as much as you do Jesus? If you do, you might be worshiping an idol. This is why Jesus said the most important commandment is to "Love the Lord your God with all your heart and with all your soul and with all your mind" (Matthew 22:37).

God has to be number one, and nothing should be a close second.

You must guard your heart. There are idols scattered all through the land, trying to steal your attention and devotion. God the Father is the only One worthy of ALL the devotion that can come from your heart.

Live Loud
ACTION

Time to do a heart-check. First, pray and ask God to show you if anything has become an idol in your life. Second, write down anything besides school, homework, sleep, and eating (i.e., the normal stuff) that gets more than one half-hour a day of your time. Third, ask your mom or dad if they think it is an idol of some sort to you, keeping you from a stronger walk with God. Fourth, make the necessary adjustments to destroy the idol.

Live Loud
THOUGHT

"Do not worship any other god, for the LORD, whose name is Jealous, is a jealous God" (Exodus 34:14).

Live God LOUD

What is a friend? A friend is someone you enjoy so much that you want to be with him or her whenever you can. A friend is someone to whom you are committed. A friend listens. A friend defends you. A friend sticks with you no matter what.

Most teens want to develop a few deep friendships. But who's got the time to do it? With all the distractions competing for your time, you're severely limited in your ability to truly connect with people. There are just too many high-tech toys, computers, stereos, cars, TVs . . . stuff. The problem is that many teens spend more time with stuff than they do with people.

Consequences of Bad Friendships

While having shallow (or no) friendships is one problem, bad friendships can be worse. They can lead you away from God, confuse you, and make you become someone on the outside that you're not on the inside. One bad friendship can wreck your entire future. "Do not be misled: 'Bad company corrupts good character'" (1 Corinthians 15:33). This means we need to really think about whom we choose to hang out with. It's rare that we just accidentally find a friend who will help us live God loud. We have to actively seek him or her out.

If you've come to the Lord recently, you've probably faced some very real friendship dilemmas. The temptation to go back and hang out with your old friends was probably your first big test. The noise from these friends can easily drown out what God may be trying to do in your life. The pressure to do the things you used to do is strategically applied to see if your new faith in Christ is simply a passing religious experience or the real thing. My old friends thought that Jesus was just a phase I'd grow out of. (Boy, were they wrong!)

Maybe you've been a Christian for a while and have made a recent decision to start living God loud. Your temptation is getting sucked back in with your halfhearted Christian friends at youth group. You know, the ones who sit in the back and make fun of everyone who really wants to seek God. If you're wondering why you keep going up and down in your walk with God, you could point to your lukewarm friends.

It is incredibly important to make new friendships with strong believers once you have completely committed your life to Jesus. You might need to end a friendship, or at least quit hanging around with those who are not saved and who are bringing you down. You may also have to stop spending time with those who are only halfhearted in their walk with God. The old friends probably will not understand why you are doing it, but God will.

Levels of Friendships

To understand friendship, we have to grasp the different levels.

Acquaintances. You know these people, and you may even refer to them as friends. You may have gone to the same classes with them for years, but the fact is, you really know nothing more about them than their name. Believe it or not, these people usually have a lot of influence on you even though you actually aren't very close to them.

Social friendships. This is where the majority of teens get stuck with a majority of their friendships. The problem is, the true loyalty factor is practically nonexistent. Though you might hang out with them at school, play sports with them, or even go to youth group together, you have more of an artificial closeness with them than something real.

I see this kind of friendship in youth groups. The teens go to camp together, have cookouts together, and meet in the same room for youth group meeting every Wednesday night for years. They sing "Kum Ba Yah" and "Friends Are Friends Forever," and everyone gets goose bumps. Some cry together at the altar every chance they get. But the truth is, they hardly know each other.

Gangs all over North America have social friendships, though the goals of the group are obviously different. They think they are close because they dress the same way and hang out together. While they claim, "I got his back," and while they *do* fight for each other, if they really cared about the other members, they'd do what they could to get them out of the situation they're in.

Close friends. Time is the key element. There may be only a few people at the end of your life whom you would classify as "close friends." The reason? True friendship requires that you drop your guard and let someone know you for who you really are. This isn't easy, due to the masks we're forced to wear most of the time. While I wish these types of friends were the norm in youth groups, it's not easy being gut-level honest with others. You never know what they might do with sensitive information you divulge about yourself.

Christians should have the best possibility for developing close friends since by definition Christians have already admitted they're not perfect, acknowledged they need Jesus Christ as their Savior, and are in agreement that life is meant to be lived devoted to serving Him.

In-this-till-the-end friends. This is the highest form of friendship known to mankind. You'll see it most with men who have been through battle together and have trusted each other with their lives. For Christians, this is the type of relationship that can end up changing the world. Paul and Silas had it. Moses and Aaron had it. Elijah and Elisha had it. Jonathan and David had it.

Jonathan and David: How They Did It

Let's look at the ingredients that made Jonathan and David's friendship special:

They had a passion to live on the edge for God. Jonathan was the kind of guy who had a lot of guts and wanted to do something for God. First Samuel 14 tells the story of how the Israelites were surrounded by the Philistines out in the middle of nowhere. Jonathan saw that all the other soldiers (about six hundred of them) were scared and confused, and he did not want to be one of them. He took his armorbearer and said, "Let's go and look at those guys and just see what happens. Maybe God will act on our behalf" (paraphrase of verse 6).

Jonathan had the courage to live on the edge for God, even if it meant risking his life for Him. But he also had a problem. He was hanging out with an army of men who were a bunch of yellow-bellied, thumb-sucking babies! He knew he couldn't have real friendships with guys who were cowards.

Then one day, he came across another battlefield. Again it pitted the Israelites against the Philistines, but this time the Philistines had a Goliath fighting on their side. All of a sudden Jonathan saw a seventeen-year-old guy with a rock in his slingshot ready to take on the giant. As you know, David hit Goliath in the head and killed him (see 1 Samuel 17). But that was not good enough. Just like a normal teenager, David wanted to do something to really make the point. So he cut off Goliath's head and brought it to the king.

I can just imagine how excited Jonathan was to find someone who had the guts to stand up for the Lord. *Finally,* he must have thought, *here is someone who has my same desire to do something big for God.* First Samuel 18:1 says Jonathan became "one in spirit with David."

They served each other and wanted each other's best. First Samuel 18:1 says Jonathan and David looked out for each other's good before their own. In 1 Samuel 20:8, David referred to himself as Jonathan's servant. In fact, at the end of 1 Samuel 20, we see a remarkable example of this attitude.

King Saul (Jonathan's dad) told Jonathan that as long as David was alive Jonathan would never be king (because the people liked David so much). He wanted Jonathan to bring David to him so he could kill him. Jonathan refused. He would NOT betray his friend even if it meant he would not be the next king. This is true SELFLESSNESS!

As a Christian, you have the best possibility of being this kind of friend, because you know that God looks out for you and that you do not have to look out for number one anymore. You can genuinely be happy when a brother or sister gets blessed in some way by God. You never feel jealousy because you want the best for them. Jesus said, "Greater love has no one than this, that he lay down his life for his friends" (John 15:13).

A few years ago, I learned that a friend of mine named Kirk Pankratz, the director of another youth ministry called Youth America, had been given the money to buy an old airport. He was going to convert it into a compound for his summer camp. I was so excited for him. Even though I had been asking God for years for a compound for Teen Mania Ministries, and it would have been easy to get jealous of Kirk, instead I had true joy in my heart that he was getting to see his dream come true. (It wasn't long afterwards that God made my dream come true by finding Teen Mania the perfect facility for our ministry in Lindale, Texas.)

They were committed to an accountability friendship. First Samuel 18:3–4 describes the kind of commitment Jonathan and David made: "And Jonathan made a covenant with David because he loved him as himself. Jonathan took off the robe he was wearing and gave it to David, along with his tunic, and even his sword, his bow and his belt."

This signified that they had made a promise to stick with each other until the end and help each other succeed. This is called "accountability friendship," and it's characterized by making a commitment to help each other grow in the Lord. It is a commitment to push each other to get closer to God. It even gives your friend permission to get in your face if you're straying from the path.

When you make this kind of commitment, you tell your friend, "I'm going to help you live God loud like you told me you wanted." It means that you say, "I love you too much to let you backslide, sin, compromise, or mess up your life." It's hard to backslide if someone cares enough by asking every day, "How was your quiet time with God today?"

In this level of friendship, you share your greatest fears and really pray for each other. You are determined to live God loud and change the world together.

⏮ ⏮ ⏮ ⏮

Is it time for you to get a friendship like this? It's impossible to live God loud with a bunch of shallow friendships (especially if some of these friends are not even Christians). You are going to have to bring your friends up to your level of commitment or find a few close friends who already are. It is time to let someone get in your face. It is time to get an "accountability friendship."

Here are some things you can commit to doing with your accountability friend:

◎ Pray for each other. Really listen to what your friend is going through and seek God together for each other.

◎ Do a similar Bible study together and commit to finishing it.

◎ Ask each other, "How was your time with the Lord today?" (And give each other the freedom to say, "Not so hot." You can't have great days every day!)

◎ Plan to change the world together this year (for example, go on a mission trip or reach a few friends for Christ at your school).

◎ Plan to stick together for at least one year and serve each other with a selfless attitude.

Find your "in-it-till-the-end friend" today. I guarantee that this person, more than anything else in your life, will help you grow in the Lord.

◄◄ *It's impossible to live God loud with a bunch of shallow friendships. . . . You are going to have to bring your friends up to your level of commitment or find a few close friends who already are.*

ACTION
Live Loud

Fill out the following pledge with a committed friend:

> ### Accountability Friendship Pledge
>
> I commit to being a "**COMMITTED, COURAGEOUS, I'M-IN-THIS-TILL-THE-END FRIEND.**" I will keep all five of the below commitments with you.
>
> Date:_____
>
>
> _____
> Signed (your name)
>
>
> _____
> Signed (friend's name)
>
> 1. Listen to each other and pray for each other.
> 2. Do the same Bible study together and commit to finishing it.
> 3. Ask each other every day, "How was your time with God today?"
> 4. Change the world together this year.
> 5. Stick with each other for at least one year and serve each other with a selfless attitude.

Live Loud
THOUGHT

"A man of many companions may come to ruin, but there is a friend who sticks closer than a brother" (Proverbs 18:24).

FIVE

◎ *Living Something That Counts*

I want to do something that matters."

"I need something to sink my life into."

"I'd give anything for my life to make a difference."

These are the things I hear teens all over America saying. It is not enough just to have fun during your teen years. It is not enough to have all the high-tech toys you could possibly imagine. There must be something more.

There is.

God has an incredible plan for you to be involved in changing the world. God isn't preparing you to be some fake Hollywood hero chasing treasure; He has a REAL mission for you.

It will demand your all.

It will push you out of your comfort zone.

It may cost you all you have, including your own plans you have made for your life.

It will give you the greatest rewards.

It will be the most adventure you could possibly imagine.

It will be more fun than a human should be allowed to have on earth.

It's God's big plan for you.

These last few chapters will keep you from EVER having a boring Christian life again. God has something big laid out for you!

⏮ *God has an incredible plan for you to be involved in changing the world. God isn't preparing you to be some fake Hollywood hero chasing treasure; He has a REAL mission for you.*

Live God LOUD

Chapter 18 ◎ Can I Really Make My Life Count for Eternity? Finding Your Purpose in the Cause

Many teenagers today are looking for something to really pour their lives into. They see all the things their parents have invested in and they're not drawn to pursue the same dream. Their parents have lived and worked for that third car, a vacation home, a boat . . . yet they're still not happy. A lot of teenagers have all the toys they could possibly want, yet their family has either no direction or is falling apart. As a result, there are millions of young followers of Christ who recognize that getting "stuff" is a pursuit that will eventually leave them empty. The shallowness of just having things isn't worthy of a life that has been redeemed by the King of kings.

Where are you?

Do you want a purpose you can really sink your teeth into? Something that will demand your all? Something that you know deep in your heart is worth doing?

Purpose gives you a reason to get out of bed every morning. It is hard to have a sense of purpose when you are going to a mundane job every day just trying to inch your way up the ladder and looking out for "Numero Uno." Find what you were born to do.

God created you to do something great for His kingdom!

When you get hold of His purpose for your life, you will finally find the abundance that Jesus promised in John 10:10 when He said, "I have come that they may have life, and have it to the full."

Getting involved in a cause isn't new to this world. Millions have thought that if they could get into something that was helping others or protest something that was bad, their existence would be justified. The fact is, God *already* has a cause for you. Actually, it is THE CAUSE. When you find your purpose in THE CAUSE, you really discover what you were born to do. And there is nothing like getting involved in the biggest CAUSE in the history of mankind!

As a teenager, I wanted to do something big for God. I wanted to minister in any meaningful way possible to people who really needed it. I thought I might be a youth pastor or a traveling minister, but nothing really seemed to fit. It wasn't big enough for the vision God wanted me to fulfill. Then I discovered THE CAUSE! It was like my eyes were opened and I could finally see the BIG PICTURE of what God wanted to do in the world through me—and through teenagers like you. It was absolutely thrilling to think that I could be involved in something so important. Instead of just talking about it, I would actually be reaching the world!

There is a place for everyone in His CAUSE, and I hope you will begin to discover yours by the end of this section.

What Is a Cause?

A cause is a response to a problem or a predicament. It demands that something be done. The problem gives you a big reason (a cause) to respond. It gives you a reason to do something loud. The problem may demand that you do more than you ever thought you could in order to be the answer to the problem.

In 1 Samuel 17, David found Israel in a predicament. Goliath had come out to challenge the army of the Lord, and no one would do anything about it. David saw the situation and cried out in verse 29, "Is there not a cause?" (KJV). He was saying, "Isn't anybody going to do something about this? Don't we have a response to this bully?" The implied answer is, "Of course we do!" David responded and killed Goliath.

God made us with the desire to pour all of our guts into something. Every human being has something in him that says, "I want to do something significant, something that matters in life, something important." That is why the Bible says, "Whatever you do, work at it with all your heart, as working for the Lord, not for men" (Colossians 3:23). The reason I've been so hard line on many issues in this book is that I know that the gadgets, temptations, distractions, and busyness of life will numb that desire, if you're not careful.

Examples of a Cause

America is plagued with people who are investing themselves in all kinds of petty causes that have no eternal value. "Save the Eels." "Save the Woodmites." "Save the Pavement." Whatever needs to be saved, some too-much-time-on-their-hands adults will take up as their "cause" in order to try to bring their life meaning.

How about teenagers? What are their "causes"? If a cause is a response to a problem, then there's a lot to crusade about, isn't there? Need more clothes? Complain to Mom and Dad, or work hard to get some new ones. Want a boyfriend or girlfriend? Go

> ◀◀ *God made us with the desire to pour all of our guts into something.*

175

on the hunt and see who's available, or tell a friend to tell a friend to tell someone you like him or her. Hey, when you're on a mission, any tactic that works you gotta try, right?

I heard of a situation in Oklahoma in which a teacher was unfairly fired from her job. Students rallied and protested. Some even went on strike and walked out of classes. Their response was, "It's not fair! She was a good teacher." They made a cause out of getting her rehired.

Others are really dismayed about cruelty to animals. As a result, there are hundreds of animal protection groups. One is called the Association for the Humane Treatment of Animals. It boasts of having 1,750,000 members.[1] Think about it. This group has 1,750,000 people involved in its cause of helping animals. Now, I am all for helping animals, but I want to help hurting people more. Could it be that it cares more about helping animals than it cares about helping hurting people? If it can get 1,750,000 people to save animals, can we not do more to save people?

Causes everywhere raise millions of dollars and rally millions of people. But the math and the value of these causes is questionable. I heard a leader from Serbia speaking on the radio during the height of the Serbian War. He said, "If one hundred thousand penguins had washed up on the shore of a beach somewhere dead, every country in the world would be there to help figure out why. We have had more than one hundred thousand people die here, and no one seems to care."

We need to begin to care about people like God does.

People are constantly trying to find purpose by pouring their lives into something. They go from cause to cause, never staying with any one cause for very long and never finding satisfaction or fulfillment. Until they find God's cause, they will run a treadmill trying to find something significant to invest their life into.

There are, of course, much-needed life-risking causes. The

wars in Vietnam, Nicaragua, and Yugoslavia were all a matter of rallying around a cause. Millions of people believed in a person or style of government so much that they were willing to die for their devotion! They put guns in their hands and said, "I am ready to kill or be killed for what I believe." If they can do that for a style of government, can we not do more for the cause of Christ?

Reporters constantly put their lives at risk for the sake of a story. I have a friend who works for CNN. He was in one of the first jeeps that drove into Kuwait after the Gulf War in 1991. He could easily have driven over land mines on the way in. He risked his life for the sake of shooting a one-minute piece of video for a news show.

I found a newspaper article about two men who were stoned to death in Somalia. They were out taking pictures one day for their newspaper. Unfortunately, they got into the wrong neighborhood and people began throwing rocks at them. After their bodies were found, they were hailed by their paper as heroes. Think about it. They gave their lives for the sake of a newspaper article! If they can do that for a newspaper that is read one day and burned the next, can we not do more for the Word of God, which will last forever?

And, of course, there are religious causes. Muslims believe so strongly in Allah that they pray five times a day at specific times no matter where they are. I saw a man in the Dallas–Fort Worth airport bow down on his knees toward Mecca and pray right in front of everyone—right in the middle of the airport!

All Buddhist young men are encouraged to be monks for three

◄◄ *Until they find God's Cause, they will run a treadmill trying to find something significant to invest their lives into.*

months of their lives. They shave their heads and walk around in orange robes begging for food for three months. They make themselves out to be complete fools, and they do something crazy for a man named Buddha who died more than a thousand years ago (and is still dead). If they can do that for someone who is still dead, can we not do more for Someone who died and rose from the dead? If they can do that for three months, can we not go one or two months to another country to share Jesus with others? (You don't even have to shave your head!)

Hindus believe that as they do things to bring pain to themselves, their gods will be pleased with them. They will walk for a week in 110-degree weather, barefoot on the pavement, to try to please their gods. They will shove a spike through their tongue or cheeks to try to get the approval of their gods. If they can do these things for the sake of gods that do not even exist (i.e., for the sake of a lie), can we not do more for the sake of the one true God?

Christians are not trying to earn something from God (unlike members of other religions). We just love Him so much that we respond by reaching out to others.

God's Cause

So what is the cause of Christ? Simple: It is people. People are what God cares about. He wants each individual in the whole world to know the truth about His Son.

Jesus put it clearly: "And this gospel of the kingdom will be preached in the whole world as a testimony to all nations, and then the end will come" (Matthew 24:14). Basically, He said the end is not coming until everyone gets a chance to hear. He is so committed to His cause that He will not allow the world to end until everyone has a chance to learn about eternal life. We can talk about Jesus coming back, pray for it, read about it, look at our watches and expect it . . . but it is not going to happen until everyone has a chance to hear the gospel.

Jesus said it this way: "My food . . . is to do the will of him who sent me and to finish his work" (John 4:34). Basically, He said, "This is My heart and passion. It is My oxygen, My drink, My food! It is all I think about! I have got to finish the task!"

God is looking for people today to get so involved that they would do anything to reach the world! He wants young people like you to get so caught up in His cause that they would do whatever it takes to help everyone know the truth.

Live Loud
ACTION

When you plug your life into the greatest CAUSE that has ever existed, you find real purpose. You find what you were born to do. You become a part of the most strategic invasion ever to hit this earth: the invasion of God's love. Since I lead a short-term mission organization, naturally I think a great way to join the cause now is to go on a mission trip. We help reach out to people who never in their lives have had a chance to hear about Jesus! Thousands of teenagers take a month or two to pour their all into something that really matters. (You can go this summer with Teen Mania Ministries. See the back of this book on how to contact us for an application for our summer or Christmas mission trips.)

You will feel an incredible sense of purpose knowing that your life is really counting for eternity!

Live Loud THOUGHT

"The men who had leprosy reached the edge of the camp and entered one of the tents. They ate and drank, and carried away silver, gold and clothes, and went off and hid them. They returned and entered another tent and took some things from it and hid them also. Then they said to each other, 'We're not doing right. This is a day of good news and we are keeping it to ourselves. If we wait until daylight, punishment will overtake us. Let's go at once and report this to the royal palace'" (2 Kings 7:8–9).

Live God LOUD

What is your dream?

What do you want to do more than anything else?

What purpose do you think your life should have?

I am afraid that too many young people are not asking themselves these questions. The reason is that too many have been discouraged and disillusioned by the negative circumstances in their lives. As you have read the different chapters in this book, you have seen that there is certainly a lot that can distract you from living God loud. But you've also seen that God has an answer for each distraction. Most of the answers are found in your choice to turn down the world and turn up God.

So now it is time to ask yourself this question: "How much do I want to live God loud, and what am I going to do with my life that will matter for eternity?"

God is looking for a generation of dreamers! He wants people who will dare to think the impossible. He is looking for young people who are ready to live on the edge for Him and do something great to change the world. It is time to stand up and take your place in history. There is no better time to start than now, when you are young. William James said, "The greatest use of life is to live it for something that will outlast it."

God is in the business of using ordinary people to do incredible things. It all starts with a dream. Every invention that was ever discovered, every ministry that was ever started, began with a dream.

If you could do anything for God, what would it be?

Proverbs 29:18 says, "Where there is no vision, the people perish" (KJV). You have got to have vision—a dream—if you want to accomplish all that God has for you. It is time to think big, pray big, and DREAM BIG!

How to Find Your Dream

Some people have been told that they "*can't*" for so long that they begin to believe it. We talked about how to overcome that feeling of helplessness and worthlessness in chapter 13. I know you have the ability to live your dreams by the mere fact that you have made it to this point of the book. You're not afraid of being challenged beyond your comfort level to consider a higher calling. You are looking for God's best.

If you are to find your dream, the first thing you need to think about is this: How does God dream? Answer: God always dreams BIG. A friend of mine says with a smile, "My God is too big to think dink." God thought of everything from the smallest chromosomes and DNA to the black holes in space when He dreamed about the universe. Psalm 92:5 says, "How great are your works, O LORD, how profound your thoughts!" When God thinks, He thinks in a big, wild, adventurous way.

The Bible says you were created in His image. That means you have the ability to think like He does (see 1 Corinthians 2:16).

> ◀◀ *God is in the business of using ordinary people to do incredible things. It all starts with a dream.*

You have a God-given ability to imagine. In fact, Genesis 2:15 says that God put Adam in the Garden of Eden to work it and to take care of it. That was Adam's job. He was to make it beautiful. He could do whatever he wanted with it except eat from the one tree. Adam used his own imagination and named the animals. God wanted him to be creative and make the garden awesome.

Proverbs 15:26 tells us that "the LORD detests the thoughts of the wicked, but those of the pure are pleasing to him." This means that if you are a Christian and walking with all your heart as close as you possibly can to Jesus, He really is pleased with what you think. Proverbs 12:5 says, "The thoughts of the righteous are right" (KJV). Let God use your thoughts—your ability to dream—to bring Him glory.

First, you should begin to dream about your personal life with Jesus. What are your goals in your relationship with the Lord? What do you really want your character to be like? How much do you want to grow in Him this next year? What areas of your life do you want transformed? In what ways do you want your prayer and Bible-reading times to get better? Dream big about your walk with the Lord.

Next, you should begin to dream about the ministry that God has for you today. What does God want to do through you this next year? How does He want to use you to change your school or workplace? What could those hangouts in your town look like in a year if you started doing something right now? What about a mission trip? Think about all the people around the world who have never had a chance to hear about Jesus— then dream big about how you could get there to reach them.

Finally, you should begin to dream about the future that God has for you. What could you really do to have a lifelong impact for the kingdom of God? How many souls could be saved? How many churches started? How much money could you pump into missions with your life of service to God? Dream big about the incredible impact your life could make.

It is not arrogant to dream big. God dreams big dreams. When you dream big, you are thinking like God would. The more creative you are, the more you imitate your heavenly Father. However, you might not want to tell everyone your dream like Joseph did (see Genesis 37). If you tell everyone, you could sound like you are puffed up. God might give you a dream, but it's not ready for everyone else to hear until you get closer to the time of actually fulfilling your dream.

Remember that He is "able to do immeasurably more than all we ask or imagine, according to his power that is at work within us" (Ephesians 3:20). That means that if you can think it, God can do it. Another pointer is never to let money or location determine your dream. You might get a great idea then think, *But how could I ever get the money to do that?* Don't you dare let money stop you! I always tell teens who want to go on a mission trip, "God has all kinds of money. You just have to find out in whose pockets He's keeping it!"

You may want to take some time right now while your ideas are fresh to write out your dreams for each of these different areas.

How to Go for It

Now that you have taken some time to write down some of the dreams that God has given you, it is time to do something about them. You must rearrange your schedule to accommodate your dreams. You have to set your priorities so that you can accomplish what you set out to do. You have to plan into your life the opportunity to execute your ideas or they will never happen.

For example, if you want to have great quiet times, you have to plan what you will do during your time with God and how much time it will take. Set time aside and plan the things necessary to put together ministry ideas that God has given you. If you do not make yourself do it, you will never reach your dreams. Fulfilling small steps to big dreams doesn't happen with the TV remote in your hand.

It is important to share your dreams with trusted friends. You need other people who believe in you, are praying for you, and are standing with you. As I said earlier, don't be like Joseph and blab it all over town, but find some trusted confidants and let them in on what God is telling you to do. People may laugh at your dreams, but if you know that God spoke them to you, then keep your head up high and keep aiming for them. A number of people laughed at me when I wanted to go across the country to share this challenge to students at colleges. Others laughed when we started Teen Mania. Still others mocked me when we set really high goals to reach the world. Today those people are not laughing anymore. I knew the dreams God had given me, and no amount of naysayers were going to distract or discourage me from them.

You have now come to the stage at which you should write out the strategy of how you are going to make your dreams happen. You have already written out the dreams. Now you have to think through all the ramifications. What should you do first? What comes next? Who else should you ask to get involved? How much will it cost? Where will you get the money? What should you do this week? This month? Each month this year? The next few years?

If God has given you a dream, then you have the responsibility to plan a way to get it done. Don't worry, God will guide you as you plan. James 1:5 says, "If any of you lacks wisdom, he

◄◄ *When you dream big, you are thinking like God would.*

should ask God, who gives generously to all without finding fault, and it will be given to him."

You might say, "I think this is God's idea, but what if it is not? I will end up doing all these things in my own strength and it will all have been a waste." Very few people hear God in an audible voice. You have to put your trust in your ability to hear Him through your spirit and through the voice of others. If you are going to err, it would be better to err by doing something where you're sharing the good news than by doing nothing. It is easier for God to steer a moving car than a parked one.

Decide to Go for It

Now that you have your dreams and your plans written out, it is time to commit. If you haphazardly try to reach your goals, you never will. Hebrews 12:2b says that "for the joy set before him [Jesus] endured the cross, scorning its shame, and sat down at the right hand of the throne of God." He always had the goal in the forefront of His mind and didn't let anything distract Him from it. He knew what the ramifications would be and was ready to do whatever it would take to accomplish His goal. He knew it would not be easy—most worthwhile things are not easy.

Are you ready to endure for your dreams? My experience has been that you need to be as resolute as Jesus was when He set out for Jerusalem (see Luke 9:51). You just need to go for it.

When God gives you a dream, it's worth giving your all for it. It is time to go for broke, lay everything on the table, and commit to doing everything in your power to accomplish your dream. Commit to Him that as long as He continues to provide and His blessing is on you, you will complete the task He has given you.

God will keep His part of the deal (He always does) if you keep your part of the deal. When it is all said and done, this world will be a different place and you will have had a lot of fun going for your dream!

Commit today to pursue your dream.

Live Loud ACTION

Hey, if you haven't got enough to do after the challenge in this chapter, your action is to reread it!

Live Loud THOUGHT

"But you will receive power when the Holy Spirit comes on you; and you will be my witnesses in Jerusalem, and in all Judea and Samaria, and to the ends of the earth" (Acts 1:8).

Live God LOUD

God has a dream for our lives. First He wants us to be "without-a-doubt" saved. Second, He wants us to be thoroughly committed to loving Him and living Him loud with all of our hearts. Third, He wants to heal the brokenness in our lives and to put us back together again. Fourth, He wants us to live clean lives and to have an undeniable passion for following His Word. The Bible says He wants to bless our lives and to give us abundant life (see John 10:10)! This is where we usually stop, but this is where He just begins.

God wants to use your life to change this world in a big way. He is thinking about you and how He desires for you to be completely strong in Him, but He is also thinking about the rest of the world. God's dream has to do with reaching the "ends of the earth" (Acts 1:8). From the beginning, He has wanted the whole world to know Him. He didn't want a part of the world; He wanted it all! He didn't want a few people; He wanted them all! He didn't just want the people in America to know Him; He wanted the whole world!

For thousands of years, God has been strategizing and orchestrating how He can get the world back. It's His dream. As humans, we think about many things. He thinks about one thing: the people of the world and how to reach them. He is specifically trying to reach those who have never had their first chance to hear about Him. His dream is that everyone would have a chance to hear.

Jonah's Mistake

Jonah, as you know if you've read the small Old Testament book that bears his name, ran from God's call on his life. God had called him to go to Nineveh, the capital of Assyria, to be a missionary. The call was the most important thing in the heart of God. He wanted Jonah to have the joy of telling people who had never had a chance to hear it the truth about what they needed to do to gain God's favor.

When Jonah decided to run from God's call, he was not simply running from a nice idea God had for him. He was trying to escape from *doing one of the most important assignments in the history of mankind!* He was trying to stand in the way of God's dream being fulfilled for a huge group of people. The Lord had even told him what to preach. He was supposed to tell them to repent or, basically, God would blow them off the face of the earth (Sodom and Gomorrah, Part Two). He didn't even have to think of his own sermon!

God always has a way of getting His job done. We know that Jonah finally showed up in Nineveh after enduring the storm and hanging out in the belly of the fish for three days. The Bible says that he preached to the people in Nineveh and everyone repented (see Jonah 3:3–5). They all fasted and put on sackcloth and ashes. Even the animals fasted! Wow, that is serious!

But Jonah was mad. He wanted to be remembered as the prophet who preached to a city that didn't repent, with the result that the whole city was destroyed. He cared more about how he looked in front of the people than he cared about the people themselves. After God had forgiven the people of Nineveh, Jonah went outside the city onto a hill to look down on the people and complain. There he was, out in the hot desertlike sun, just as mad as he could be. God decided to have some mercy on him. He grew up a plant while Jonah was sleeping so he could have some shade. Jonah woke up in the morning still angry, and he complained all day. God said, "Forget this," and when Jonah woke up the next day the plant was dead. Now Jonah was really mad!

God asked him, " 'Do you have a right to be angry about the vine?' 'I do,' he said. 'I am angry enough to die'" (Jonah 4:9). Jonah was so wrapped up in his plant, and whether he had shade, that he never caught God's heart for people. He cared more about his reputation as a prophet than about the people. He cared more about his own comfort than he did about the people.

God was trying to get Jonah to care about His dream, and all he cared about was himself. It is as if God were saying, "Jonah, can't you see? I have been trying to get you to care about all these people in Nineveh. Even after preaching to them you still missed the whole point! Shouldn't I care about them, Jonah? Of course I should, and so should you!"

It's Time!

It is time for all Christians—beginning with you and me—to start caring about God's dream for the world and not just about our own lives!

I am afraid that too many of us Christians are still like Jonah. We care more about our clothes and CD players than about reaching others. We care more about whether God has answered our prayers for a new car than whether He answered our prayers for reaching a country. We get mad when we do not have the answer and get what we want right away. "But, God, I prayed for that thing! Why isn't it here yet?" are the words God hears all too often. We are more concerned with whether we are comfortable than we are with God's passion to reach those who have never heard His gospel.

God wants us to care about what He cares about more than our own comfort. So what if we give up eating at McDonald's for a month while we go to the mission fields? (Besides, most countries have McDonald's.) So maybe you have to sleep on a harder bed for a month or two. Is it worth it to reach people? Of course it is.

God is looking for young people who will make His dream their utmost priority, people who are consumed with a passion to complete the cause they've been given as their part in God's dream.

Paul's Ambition

Paul said in Romans 15:20, "It has always been my ambition to preach the gospel where Christ was not known." Basically, he said, "I want to go where no one else wants to go. It's my passion, my heart, my soul, my everything, to go and preach where no one ever has before."

Paul just could not be happy doing what God had called other Christians to do. The job of shepherding and growing in his faith by osmosis (hanging around church picnics and youth group outings) wasn't for him. He had to do something that would change the world! God planted in Paul a burning desire to let others know about the One who had so drastically changed his life.

What are your ambitions? What are you aspiring to achieve with your life? God is looking for a generation of young people who really care about what He cares about. He wants to make

His dream our dream! Only then will we pour all our life into accomplishing the only thing that really matters.

The result of God's dream is described in Revelation 7:9: "After this I looked and there before me was a great multitude that no one could count, from every nation, tribe, people and language, standing before the throne and in front of the Lamb."

Revelation describes God's dream come true. He gets His way after all!

It does not matter what it costs; it is only God's dream that matters. It does not matter what we have to give up, where we have to move, where we have to go, how illogical it may seem, or how much everyone else may not understand; it is only God's dream that is worth pouring your life into.

Some people might think, "Come on, I just want to have a little fun! This is too serious for a teenage Christian." I'm sorry to say, but Jesus did not die so that we could have good, clean fun! He wants everyone to know Him, and it is time that we as His family start aiming at getting them all into the kingdom of God. This is a serious calling we have.

About 43 percent of the world's population is currently under twenty years of age.[1] I have discovered that it takes young people to reach young people.

Are you ready?

It is your turn to make your mark on the world for Jesus! Would you dare to go and get involved personally in making God's dream come true?

"For God so loved the world that He . . ." No, He DID NOT send an e-mail to let us know about His love. " . . . He sent His Son!" He sent a person.

Today, God still sends people. He does not simply want some of our money to go on missions; He wants US to go! He does not just want tracts and Bibles to go overseas; He wants flesh-and-blood people to go.

When you personally reach out and put your arms around those who have never heard, you will touch a little bit of His dream. When you personally look into the eyes of a man or woman who has never had a chance to hear the gospel and you watch them go from darkness to light, you make a discovery: You discover what it feels like to be involved in the most important adventure since the beginning of mankind. You are helping God's dream become a reality, and there is nothing like it!

Make plans now to do something about changing the world. Write, call, or e-mail Teen Mania Ministries (or any other missions agency you or your church might be familiar with) to get an application to go on a mission trip. (See page 197 for information on contacting Teen Mania Ministries.)

Teen Mania takes teens of all ages as well as young adults to countries around the world during summer and Christmas breaks. Right now is the time to start living God loud by living God's dream!

Live Loud ACTION

Start researching Teen Mania Ministries or other mission organizations and praying about where God would want your life to count this summer or this Christmas.

Live Loud THOUGHT

"While they were worshipping the Lord and fasting, the Holy Spirit said, 'Set apart for me Barnabas and Saul for the work to which I have called them'" (Acts 13:2).

193

Live God LOUD

Endnotes ◎

Chapter 1. Getting God's Full Meal Deal

1. Rockford Institute, *The New Research* (November 1990): 2–4.
2. *Fundamentalist Journal* (October1984).
3. Neil T. Anderson and Steve Russo, *Seduction of Our Children* (Eugene, Oreg.: Harvest House, 1991), 90.
4. *Facets* (July 1989): 1.
5. *The New Research*, 2–4.
6. *Dallas Morning News*, 11 October 1987.

Chapter 4. Developing Consistent Quiet Times

1. Patrick Johnstone, *Operation World* (Grand Rapids: Zondervan, 1993).

Chapter 5. Seven Reasons to Wait

1. "STD Hotline," *Medical Aspects of Human Sexuality* (February 1991): 60.

2. Isadore Rosenfeld, "Stay Safe and Know Your STDs," *Parade Magazine,* 8 August 2000, 8.
3. Ibid.
4. Barbara Kantrowitz, "The Dangers of Doing It," *Newsweek,* special issue, summer/fall 1990, 56–57.
5. Kim Painter, "Syphilis Cases Hit 41-Year Peak," *USA Today,* 2 February 1990.
6. "Stay Safe and Know Your STDs."
7. Ibid.

Chapter 11. Divorced Parents, Single Parents, and Stepparents

1. *Pastor's Weekly Briefing* 2, no.35 (2 September 1994).

Chapter 13. Teenage Bubonic Plague: Inferiority

1. "Teens at High Risk for Mental Illness," *USA Today*, 9 October 1990, 1D.

Chapter 14. The People behind the Tunes

1. *MTV Examined,* Reel to Real Ministries.
2. *Focus on the Family* (August 1994): 2–4.

Chapter 18. Finding Your Purpose in the Cause

1. *Encyclopedia of Associations,* 1995, 29th ed. (Detroit: Gale Research, 1994).

Chapter 20. God's Dream

1. United Nations Population Trends Division, 1990 figures.

Teen MANIA

About Teen Mania Ministries ◎

Teen Mania Ministries is all about helping young people be extreme for God. Here's what we do:

◎ **Teen Mania global expeditions.** Thousands of young people are changing the world as they travel to thirty different countries for mission trips.

◎ **Acquire the Fire youth conventions.** Teen Mania hosts weekly youth conventions across North America during which teens learn about radical Christian living.

◎ **www.acquirethefire.com.** More than nine million people visit our Web site each month. Young people surf our online devotions, chat rooms, and discussion boards.

◎ **Acquire the Fire dome events.** Each year, Teen Mania hosts a dome event that challenges teens' faith. More than 70,000 teens and leaders attended the events at the Silverdome in Pontiac, Michigan, in 1999 and 2000.

◎ **Acquire the Fire television show.** Ron Luce hosts a weekly program for teens that airs on several television outlets, such as the Trinity Broadcasting Network.

◎ **Teen Mania honor academy.** Each year, high-school graduates live on the Teen Mania campus in Garden Valley, Texas, for an exciting one-year program on faith, leadership, purpose, vision, integrity, and honor.

President and founder Ron Luce started Teen Mania Ministries with his wife, Katie, in 1986. He has traveled to more than fifty countries proclaiming the gospel of Jesus Christ. His dream is to empower young people to take a stand for Christ in their schools and in their world.